SMASH YOUR JOB MARKET COMPETITION

Career Volunteering strategies for landing your dream job, and eye-opening insights for creating a successful future!

+---+

Mark Stefanick, An Ideal Professional Speaker
For Your College Events, and "Sometime Actor"
Career Programs -- Freshmen Orientation & Welcome Week
Greek Sponsored Events -- Lectures (Anytime of Year)
Conferences To Satisfy Volunteer Requirements -- Student Leadership

To request a speaking packet or check speaking availability, contact:
1-888-670-6504 -- Speaker@ProjectSledgehammer.org
www.ProjectSledgehammer.org

+---+

Mark Stefanick, Founder
ProjectSledgehammer.org, a project of Career Volunteering

© Copyright 2003 Career Volunteering, Inc. and Mark Stefanick. All rights reserved.

No part of this publication may be reproduced, stored in a retrieval system, or transmitted, in any form or by any means, electronic, mechanical, photocopying, recording, or otherwise, without the written prior permission of the author.

Text Editing by Natalie Mangini Stefanick
Cover graphics by Mark Stefanick and Pittsburgh Filmmakers

Warning – Disclaimer
The purpose of this book is to educate and entertain. This book does not promise or guarantee that anyone following the ideas, tips, suggestions, techniques or strategies will be hired. It is the discretion of employers if you will or will not be hired. The author, publisher and distributor(s) shall have neither liability nor responsibility to anyone with respect to any loss or damage caused, or alleged to be caused, directly or indirectly by the information contained in this book.

Printed in Victoria, Canada

```
National Library of Canada Cataloguing in Publication

Stefanick, Mark
      Smash your job market competition : career volunteering strate-
gies for landing your dream job and eye-opening insights for creating
a successful future / Mark Stefanick.
ISBN 1-4120-0527-2
      I. Title.
HN49.V64S77 2003            361.3'7            C2003-903325-2
```

TRAFFORD

This book was published *on-demand* in cooperation with Trafford Publishing.
On-demand publishing is a unique process and service of making a book available for retail sale to the public taking advantage of on-demand manufacturing and Internet marketing. **On-demand publishing** includes promotions, retail sales, manufacturing, order fulfilment, accounting and collecting royalties on behalf of the author.

Suite 6E, 2333 Government St., Victoria, B.C. V8T 4P4, CANADA
Phone   250-383-6864   Toll-free   1-888-232-4444 (Canada & US)
Fax   250-383-6804   E-mail   sales@trafford.com
Web site   www.trafford.com   TRAFFORD PUBLISHING IS A DIVISION OF TRAFFORD HOLDINGS LTD.
Trafford Catalogue #03-0896   www.trafford.com/robots/03-0896.html

10   9   8   7   6   5   4   3

Contents

Acknowledgements

Foreword By Joe Martin, America's Top Motivational Professor

Introduction

Chapter One: A Lesson On Your Life's Direction. (Contributing Author: Extreme Mike McKeller)

Chapter Two: A Lesson On Initiative And Focus.

Chapter Three: A Lesson On Contributing.

Chapter Four: A Lesson On Better Questions. (Contributing Author: Tanya Brown, Nicole Brown Simpson's Youngest Sister)

Chapter Five: A Brief Lesson On Frustration.

Chapter Six: A Lesson On Doing Something. Career Volunteer As HARD As You Can.

Chapter Seven, Part A.: A Lesson On Finding An Organization To Work For.

Chapter Seven, Part B.: A Lesson On Contacting An Organization To Career Volunteer For.

Chapter Seven, Part C.: A Lesson On Career Volunteering Examples To Suggest During Your Non-Profit Interview.

Chapter Seven, Part D.: A Lesson On Organizing Your Thoughts To Get Started.

*Chapter Eight: Rules - Starting A Project Sledgehammer Group. Become a Project Sledgehammer Leader. Mentor others in or out of your curriculum to Career Volunteer as a group.

Chapter Nine: A Call To Action

Chapter Ten: A Lesson On Doing Some Problem Bashing In Your Curriculum With These National And International Organizations, Such As United Way Agencies. They Are Organized By Curriculum.

Chapter Eleven: A Lesson On A Few Interviewing Tips

Closing Remark

Career Volunteering Action Check List

Career Volunteering Survey

Bibliography

Acknowledgements

Special thanks to those who have helped me in my life:

To the everyday hero Career Volunteers that overwhelm and humble me, always.

To my wife Natalie for her patience and wonderful editing skills.

To my boys, Patrick and Daniel, for always bringing joy into my life.

To my parents (John & Dorothy) for their support with the decisions I have made and continue to make in my life.

To Joe Martin for his heartfelt talks that encouraged me to write this book.

To James Malinchak for his expert consulting which enabled me to get started speaking on the college circuit.

To Jon Linden for the many ideas that he suggested for my non-profit.

To Dennis Widmyer, Kevin Kölsch and Parker Cross for my shot at "madness and loss" with the feature film, OUR LADY OF SORROW - www.OurLadyOfSorrow.com.

To Paul Sinclair – www.1world1people.org, and Korak Day – www.KorakDay.com who have held sick and dying AIDS patients in their arms, not letting them die alone. Their work has encouraged me to keep my heart in the right place.

To Raphael Pantalone for lending his smashing artistic talents to my Public Service Announcement at www.ProjectSledgehammer.org/psa.mpg, and with my caricature in this book.

To Chuck Palahniuk for writing the novel FIGHT CLUB, which was most influential to me. I believe that Project Sledgehammer and FIGHT CLUB share the same philosophy of sacrificing oneself for the greater good while offering alternatives to avoid excessive materialism in an empty consumer culture.

To contributing authors, Extreme Mike McKeller and Tanya Brown.

Lastly, to "staff hungry" national non-profit organizations that have a local presence in our communities, and make our communities stronger.

Forward By Real World Professor, Joe Martin

One of the most emotional times for a college professor is when a student -- who's a senior - finally graduates and leaves to enter the "real world." I'm sure it's an equally emotional time for parents as well, but for professors, we know that we may not ever get a chance to see or communicate with these students again. However, for me personally, the lack of future communication doesn't really concern me - although it would be nice if some would call once in a while. But more importantly, I'm concerned whether or not my graduating seniors are professionally prepared to enter the "real world."

At the beginning of each semester, I always ask my graduating seniors, "How many you have gotten internships or some type of cooperative education position?" To my amazement, less than 10% usually raise their hands. I then find myself frantically trying to cram "real world" experience into a 16-week course, so 90% of my students will at least appear to be competent when they enter the work place.

How important is it for students to get internships, volunteer, or co-op, BEFORE they graduate? Basically, I believe it's more important than graduating with honors or at the top of your class. As a professor, I try my best to use real-world examples, role play, bring in outside speakers, assign interview projects with "real" professionals, etc. However, nothing, and I mean absolutely nothing replaces actual hands-on, "I've-been-there-done-that" work experience.

I've learned from writing hundreds of recommendation letters for students that employers are quite forgiving of poor grades, but they are painfully less forgiving of a lack of work experience - especially when another job candidate has it. Like a famous politician once said, if you prepare yourself for an opportunity - i.e., get practical work experience, maintain good grades, get involved in student activities, and network with your professors - you will always make it difficult for a potential employer to say, "We like you, BUT..."

So, my advice to you is GET an internship, volunteer, and/or co-op immediately, like CAREER VOLUNTEERING! Don't wait until the last minute, or your graduation day may actually become a burden instead of a blessing. And when you graduate, make sure there aren't any "BUTS" on you resume.

In spite of being reared in one of the toughest inner-city ghettos in Miami, Florida, **Joe Martin** started his first business at age 22 and his second at age 26. He became the youngest, tenured-earning faculty member ever hired to teach at a state university in Florida at the age of 24. He is a national award-winning speaker, university professor, author, and educational consultant. Joe has a master's degree in communication, has worked as a sales trainer for a Fortune 500 company, and held a position as Communications Director for the Florida Governor's Office. Currently, Joe teaches public relations at the University of West Florida in Pensacola, Florida, and lectures on more than 50 college campuses a year. Joe Martin is the Founder and President of Real World University and can be reached at: www.RWUuniversity.com

Introduction

Welcome to Project Sledgehammer, a project of Career Volunteering. The first rule about Project Sledgehammer is you talk about Project Sledgehammer. The Second Rule about Project Sledgehammer is you TALK about Project Sledgehammer. 1 My name is Mark Stefanick, and I want to help you break through the obstacles in your life to help you reach your maximum potential.

I want to help you succeed because I am passionate about helping young adults figure out what they want to do with the rest of their lives, especially while living in these turbulent times. The media constantly reports stories of senseless violence and lives being lost. Here's a chance for young adults to help others and in many cases to actually save lives with Project Sledgehammer! Here's a chance for young adults to be involved in something larger than themselves. I decided that involving young adults as everyday heroes with Project Sledgehammer can prod the human race to evolve ONE person at a time. I believe that people like you are the glue of society because you show a desire to join Project Sledgehammer and make a difference. You're just in time to help because I believe that American Culture is in decline. Are we not experiencing a pampered, overindulgence, orgy era like was witnessed in history during the fall of Rome?

      Learn from history so we don't keep making the same mistakes.
      Make history, don't just be a part of it.
      How will history remember you?
      Learn from my mistakes.

Think about it, if people cannot decide what they want to do in life, the ramifications of their mediocrity and sheepishness have a good chance of perpetuating to their children and possibly their children's children. If you are not satisfied with your life, how can you possibly satisfy others in your life? Falling into the trap of merely living comfortably is not evolving, and eventually will sabotage your chances of genuine success.

Society programs us to think that buying some happiness, that buying a new car, a nice home with modern conveniences and accoutrements, and dish or cable T.V. is REALLY living. I mean, what is the point of stretching yourself, making sacrifices or taking chances if you are distracted by the perception that you have it all. You don't. In fact, the most successful people I know hardly had anything growing up. They clawed and climbed their way out of poverty, started a business that they truly enjoy and never looked back. Not having much not only made them hungry for life's opportunities, but the absence of some luxuries offered less distraction in pursuit of their goals. If you tune out all the fluff and focus on the one or two specific things that you want to accomplish professionally, the money will take care of itself.

Ever since our sugarcoated view of the world was blown away on 9/11/01, the sentiment was that people wanted to do something to help in their communities. Brutally clear events in United States history tend to unify and bring out the best in people, but many young Americans still haven't quite figured out how they are going to contribute. For instance, take a good look around campus in your everyday life at what your friends and others are doing. Would you not agree that even after 9/11/01, many young adults are still lazy, self-absorbed, and have a "Here we are now, entertain us" 13 attitude? That's ok. Be **thankful** for lazy people and heed an important piece of advice: DO the OPPOSITE of what they are doing, and your small accomplishments will seem stellar in comparison. Doing the opposite and going against the grain may require some effort, but it's worth it especially because of increased competition in a tight job market. If you are competing against your friends, make it a friendly competition. Challenge your friends to do the opposite too.

All systems check.
Success breeds success.
Do some PROBLEM BASHING.
Follow the path to self-discovery.
Project Sledgehammer: HEAVY METAL for your resume and your life!
Fill your life with meaningful goals and experiences, not excuses.

I decided to take back some control and help young adults make their communities stronger with Project Sledgehammer, a project of Career Volunteering. I felt obligated to give something back and sacrifice myself for the greater good because I have lived on easy street all my life. In fact, my brother nicknamed me "Average" because I've led such a normal, comfortable life. I now feel that I would be ashamed if I weren't involved with something larger than myself. Point is, I do not live in fear of my life or in an oppressed socialist or communist regime. And I certainly don't take the men and women who serve and die for our country for granted anymore because it is their sacrifice that allows our freedom to flourish. I mean, I've **never** been shelled or shot at. Life's been too comfortable, and I feel like doing some problem BASHING. The best way to honor those who have freely given their blood for our freedom is to seek the truth, tenaciously pursue excellence, preserve the United States Constitution and evolve.

Fight for your country, YOUR community with Project Sledgehammer.
"Freedom works. Freedom is the baseline for the human condition."-Jim Quinn
Life is precious.
"Life was meant to be spent, not saved." - Joe Martin
You never know when your time will be up on this Earth.

Perhaps you feel the same way I do, that volunteering is personally very gratifying, and that you want to hammer away at our problems and be a force for change during troubled times. After all, is the human race evolving with the excesses and conveniences of today? I don't think so. "You have a class of young strong men and women, and they want to give their lives to something. Advertising has these people chasing cars and clothes they don't need. Generations have been working in jobs they hate, just so they can buy what they don't really need. We don't have a great war in our generation, or a great depression, but we do, we have a great war of the spirit. We have a great revolution against the culture. The great depression is our lives. We have a spiritual depression... This is your life and it's ending one minute at a time... quit treading water and do something with our lives." 1

When was the last time that you REALLY felt good about doing something, about doing anything? If you GIVE back by Career Volunteering, you GET a quality achievement on your resume. If enough of us come together and focus on helping others, even if we are helping ourselves during the process, we still may be able to achieve at least some Peace on Earth.

Shouldn't we live each day to the fullest as if it were our last, while commanding a purpose and direction? The ancient Greeks had only one question for you before you died, "Did you live your life with passion?" Similarly, James Dean said, "Dream as if you'll live forever. Live as if you'll die tomorrow." I am confident that this book can be an affirmation on how to live passionately while helping you find your way.

    Look to yourself as an uber Career Volunteer.
    Career Volunteer as HARD as you can.
    Do it for yourself. Do it for something larger than yourself.
    Start a Project Sledgehammer Group. See Chapter Eight.
    Enjoy the process. Do the work. Have fun in your group.
    "Stay the **course**." 22
    In all likelihood, earn college **course** credits!
    Satisfy any volunteer requirements well before graduating.

I think you will find that this book is a mix of inspiration, motivation, personal stories and goal setting, yet offers you Career Volunteering opportunities in pursuit of "self-directing" your life and maximizing your career potential. 14 Feel free to pick through the chapters in this book "cafeteria style," and pick out what is important to you. It's worth it if you get one idea from this book! While reading, ask yourself, "How do you see yourself helping?" Take notes throughout this book. This is not your usual classroom note taking. The prophetic notes that you write in this book could become your plan in life.

I have faith that you can develop a sense of urgency and look to yourself to accomplish your goals in life, but never forget that there is nothing more important than your good health, family & friends, and rewarding experiences in life.

Chapter One: A Lesson On Your Life's Direction

Why is it that the majority of the student body, even from the best universities, end up with some sort of dissatisfaction with their lives? You probably won't be surprised to see many lethargic zombies trudging listlessly through life. Brother, that is the look of dissatisfaction. Seinfeld said that you can tell someone has completely given up when they wear sweatpants in public!

So why do a lot of people lead disappointing lives? How does the disappointment start? Well, in all my years of formal education, I have not had one class on how to set goals... In other words, these people **don't plan to fail, they fail to plan.** I was taught the usual subjects, but it was left to me to identify my talents and discover my career path. General counseling is offered to students; however, the difference is that there are only a few coordinators trying to individually serve the hundreds or thousands of the student population. Of course, numerous young adults simply don't want to learn and want to live only for the moment. It's a shame that most schools counseling programs are stalled simply because of the low faculty to student ratio. And what if your counselor doesn't like their job? Will they really be passionate to help you? Let's hope that most of them are.

There are obvious distinctions between those who achieve lasting success and those who fail. Winners value the power of information, whether through life changing experience or by published knowledge, and have a plan. Those who worry about the future haven't found and thus applied the information that's available to them. They invariably lack focus, initiative, have feelings of insecurity or uncertainty in themselves and may experience trouble in making decisions. I'm glad that you are reading my book because I also read a lot of the latest books about personal development. I followed the adage that if you put good things into your mind, eventually good things will have to start coming out. I fed my mind with books and audio programs from such authors as: Joe Martin, James Malinchak, Brian Tracy, Tony Robbins, Wess Roberts, Earl Nightingale, Og Mandino, Kenneth Blanchard, and Harvey MacKay. One of my favorites was LEADERSHIP SECRETS OF ATTILA THE HUN by Wess Roberts. Attila on choosing your enemies says, "Do not make enemies who are not worthy of your efforts to render them completely ineffective." That was a valuable idea. When I finish an entire program, and it generates just one applicable idea, it was worth the cost to me.

I couldn't imagine a world without arts and entertainment. Diversions like music, novels, art, nature, sports, and films influence our direction in life.

We are motivated by the feelings of anger and frustration in many of the songs that we hear.

Novels may offer positive influences. Recommended reading: FIGHT CLUB, RICH DAD POOR DAD, and THE ART OF WAR.

T.V. shows let us laugh and forget about being so serious all the time.

Talk radio is useful to call into and debate a wide spectrum of issues and topics like politics and current events.

And many films impact our ideology.

Some stories are fictional.

Some stories are real.

Everybody likes a hero.

Spectator sports can be a constructive diversion as evidenced by the following quote from Condoleezza Rice, Bush Administration national security adviser. On her dream job as NFL Commissioner she says, "I think it would be a very interesting job because I actually think football, with all due respect to baseball, is a kind of national pastime that brings people together across social lines, across racial lines. And I think it's an important American institution." Participating in sports like my high school's rifle marksmanship team offered responsibility, teamwork and leadership. Even trying out for a sport can serve as a learning experience. For instance, I tried out for my high school's golf team. On the first hole I was so nervous that I hit two drives into a pond. I crushed the third down the center of the fairway, but ultimately took a quadruple bogey. Seeing my "agony of defeat" on the first hole, a player in my group displayed brilliant sportsmanship. He reminded me of the fact that we were playing match and not stroke play. I didn't make the golf team, but a kind word from my fellow competitor interrupted my painfully embarrassing train of thought after a horrible start. To this day, if I am having a bad or challenging day, I interrupt my state of mind by thinking about people who have had real life or death challenges in their lives.

Take **Michael "Extreme Mike" McKeller** for example. Extreme Mike is a nationally recognized speaker and expert on overcoming obstacles and controlling fear. He has appeared on numerous talk shows and been interviewed in various publications and on TV, such as CNN-International, CNN Headline News and the CNN School Network. McKeller also has an Emmy nominated adventure shows that aired on PBS. For more information, please visit his website at www.ExtremeMike.com. Extreme Mike was gracious to write this passage about being thankful.

Extreme Mike says, "I'm often asked in my speaking engagements, 'Are you angry at having a disability?' It's an interesting question because it shows me that some people can't quite grasp that I actually have a very good life. They seem to expect me to be like the stereotypical disabled person - hostile, angry and antisocial. As my friends and family can attest, my attitude is 180 degrees from that. Sure, there are times I get angry and frustrated at the cards I've been dealt, but those moments are usually brief and infrequent. Anger and hostility are negative emotions that actually work against me, so I keep them in check. Of course I'd rather not have the physical challenges I deal with, but frankly I've found many things to be thankful for as a result of the disability. I've learned valuable lessons that I may not have learned without the difficulties I've faced, and I've met wonderful people who I may not have met - most people with some type of impairment would echo this as well. For one thing, life can always be worse so it makes sense to appreciate what you do have, no matter what it is you're dealing with.

Most obstacles we face are merely speed bumps, ones that will be behind us shortly if we allow them to be; dwelling on them doesn't help. And all obstacles are an opportunity to become more creative and patient. There have been few challenges I've faced that determination, creativity and lots of patience couldn't overcome. My belief is that the pain of struggle is temporary, but the pain of quitting is permanent - so don't EVER quit or give up. Controlling fear, and using it as a learning tool, has been one of the most valuable lessons for which I am thankful. Though I use a wheelchair and have limited strength and dexterity, I've been able to accomplish goals that I may never have even attempted without the disability and learning those lessons. For example, I learned to SCUBA dive though I couldn't swim, I went skydiving though I couldn't stand, started several successful businesses, and the list goes on… The most important lessons I'm grateful to have learned are to build on what one does have, to expand one's horizons and to make life an adventure. If you will consider that you alone have control over your attitude, then you alone have control over your happiness. As the adage says, 'Your attitude determines your altitude.' "

I certainly do not take for granted what I have. I am thankful to have good health, a good family, and I enjoy what I do to earn a living. Even America's poor are viewed as rich by the rest of the third world, who truly live in REAL poverty. Many of America's poor have adequate shelter, food, cable T.V., Internet access and perhaps a car. I would not want to live trapped lives like America's poor, but they do live in luxury compared with the real poor and starving of our world. Sometimes I think about how Christ suffered for us or I reflect on the millions who gave their lives for our freedom.

I think about the rallying call of Todd Beamer's "Let's roll," as he became one of the first soldiers in the War On Terrorism. He was a heroic passenger on Flight 93 during 9.11.01 that crashed not but 45 miles from my home in Pennsylvania and prevented the jet from crashing into its Washington D.C. target.

During the Civil War, many immigrants just getting off the boat immediately enlisted with the North (See the film GANGS OF NEW YORK) because they had known only persecution and injustice in their homeland, and knew that freedom was worth fighting for. While reflecting on their sacrifice, amazingly, my petty concerns pale in comparison, and "…everything in the real world gets the volume turned down." 1

    Christ suffered on the cross for my salvation.
    Billy Yank took a bullet in the gut preserving the Union.
    Rosie The Riveter feverishly assembled WWII Sherman Tanks.
    "Without pain and sacrifice we would be nothing." ibid

I never had an interest in The American Civil War (1861-1865), until I happened to catch the A&E Network's CIVIL WAR JOURNAL. Civil War battlefield medicine was the topic. Many Civil War Generals studied the warfare tactics of France's self-proclaimed conqueror and emperor, Napoleon Bonaparte (1769-1821). Napoleonic tactics were to march to the enemy in tidy, disciplined battle lines, deliver their fire, and finally charge the enemy to give them the bayonet. Typically, Northern and Southern armies followed the same tactics, except Napoleon's Army was armed with SMOOTHBORE muskets that shot lead balls, which had an effective range of about 50 yards. Civil War soldiers were armed with .58 caliber, RIFLED muskets that fired a Minié ball.

The soft lead Minié ball was cone shaped with a hollow base. When the musket was discharged, the exploding black powder forced the grooved, outside edges of the hollow base against the barrel's rifling. Not only did this improve the efficiency of the exploding gas, but it also spun the bullet. This new, aerodynamic, spinning bullet that pierced the air was very accurate up to 350 yards, and had a killing range of almost a half-mile. The Minié ball proved devastating when great Civil War armies clashed. It was not like a modern day high velocity bullet that would either clip or pierce bone. The Minié ball weighed up to 1 1/2 ounces, traveled slower was hard to stop and the hot lead hit flesh and bone like a sledgehammer.

  You can say, "Searing flesh and splintered bone."
  You can say, "Amputation," if you're lucky.
  You can say, "Lethal," if you're not.

Men with a gut shot didn't have a chance and were left to die under the shade of a tree, known as the dying tree. The damage to human tissue, cartilage, arteries, veins and bones was overwhelming. Bones were shattered, could not be dealt with surgically and limbs were amputated. The fact that the Minié ball had caused countless amputations peaked my macabre psyche's interest enough to become a Civil War enthusiast. I have read many books, collected videos, and visited most of the major battlefields in the East. I also watched a North South Skirmish Association (NSSA) shooting event, in which NSSA uniformed Union and Confederate teams, representing actual historical units, compete in live musket, carbine, revolver, and artillery marksmanship. The best part was cannon target competition. I learned that cannons were accurate up to about a mile. It's hard to imagine what kind of courage it took to charge dozens of cannon.

  I learned a great deal about the mettle and leadership of the men and women on both sides of the Civil War, and it changed me as a person. History taught me about a man who came from a middle class background, who didn't have to sacrifice himself for the greater good, but did. Joshua Lawrence Chamberlain could have sat out the Civil War with a cushy professorship at Bowdoin College in Brunswick, Maine, but didn't. Chamberlain took command of the 20th Maine prior to marching into Gettysburg, PA on July 1, 1863, which was the first bloody day of three during the Battle of Gettysburg. On the second day, Chamberlain's regiment was ordered to Little Round Top to protect the Union left flank. If Chamberlain's regiment collapsed, the whole Union Army could be routed in a panic.

  The 20th Maine was attacked on the afternoon of July 2, 1863. The ensuing battle lasted for hours and was a bloody tug of war. With his men spent, and with ammunition just about out, his greatest moment was at hand. He knew that if his men were about to break, the Confederates were also on the brink. The idea came quickly to Chamberlain. He ordered, "Fix bayonets!" Next he roared, "Charge bayonets!" Finally, he erupted, "CHARGE!" The 20th Maine was unleashed and devastatingly smashed into the Confederates downhill. The Confederates were horrified by the bayonet attack, and hundreds were killed or captured. The 20th Maine prevented the Union left flank from crumbling. Ultimately, Chamberlain was awarded the Congressional Medal of Honor for his heroism at Gettysburg. It was inspiring to see a soft-spoken man living a comfortable life sacrifice it all for the cause of preserving the Union and freeing the slaves. When I learned about Chamberlain, I decided that I was going to devote my life to something larger than myself with Project Sledgehammer.

"Is there nothing left
Is there, is there nothing
Is there nothing left
Is honesty what you want
A generation without name, ripped and torn
Nothing to lose, nothing to gain
Nothing at all
And if you can't help yourself
Well take a look around you
When others need your time
You say it's time to go... it's your time" 16

Some young adults are lucky to have a mentor in their lives to help them with their future. Mentors may enter into your life where you least expect it. They could be a coach, a neighbor, a teacher, a family member, an officer, a business owner or somebody that you don't expect. During high school, I met my mentor, Charlie, at a pizza place where my friend Mike worked. Charlie's travel agency was adjacent to the pizza shop and he'd occasionally come in for a pie. He'd entertain us by throwing steak knives into the ceiling when the owner wasn't around. Here was a brawny guy with a suit and tie darting out of the way so the falling steak knives wouldn't impale him. How could I not like the guy? I befriended him. We generally pestered each other because he had a twisted sense of humor. Eventually, I asked Charlie if I could work for him the next summer after my freshman year in college since I was going to be a marketing major. He said to contact him. The following summer I met with him and asked for the internship. He said that he really didn't take me seriously when I originally asked him, but was IMPRESSED that I followed through. I got the summer job, which led to working part-time from my college apartment and full-time during the next few summers. He taught me so much about business and marketing, and I am grateful for the learning experience.

Others draw, paint, write, dance, compete athletically or sing their way towards a better future. Sometimes we are driven to create and express ourselves out of necessity to cope with the loss of a parent, sibling, close family member or friend.

A negative experience certainly can be a learning experience. During college, I pledged a social fraternity. Initially it was fun because of the parties and mixers with sororities. The hazing wasn't that bad. See... Run to the convenience store for a fraternity brother while being timed. Also see... late nights. Also see... late nights locked up in an attic. Also see... act as bouncer even if an unruly guest pulls a knife on you. By the way, the knife-wielding degenerate was too drunk to take advantage of his weapon and was pummeled.

This fraternity encouraged academic excellence and encouraged general type volunteering. However, there was a dark, seedy side to some of its members that I will always remember. The most disturbing example occurred in the cafeteria where pledges had to sit facing the wall so the brothers could keep an eye on the action and girls in the packed hall. Brother Jim, who I originally thought was a stand up guy, tells me to turn around and look at a plainly dressed guy who paused while searching for a seat. As I turned around, Jim starts berating him with insults like, "Look at him, what a f*cking geek, what a f*cking loser." And he ended with something to the effect that his kind should be dragged out and shot. It got so quiet in the hall that you could hear green Jell-O drop on the floor until Jim and the rest of the brothers burst out laughing. Like an instinctual reflex, I picked up my tray and left the table. I marched over to the frat house, explained what had happened to the chapter president, who was also my big brother, and de-pledged. He shrugged it off as immature behavior and asked me to forget about it and stay. I resisted and went against the grain. I explained that the student on the receiving end of Brother Jim's tirade in front of the entire cafeteria must have been extremely humiliated and probably had his confidence shattered for a long time to come. I said that I didn't want to be a part of any organization where its members bully or prey upon those who are weaker than them. Besides, this student looked like Bill Gates, and I thought that someday Jim might end up working for the same guy he publicly thrashed. At that point, payback would be a bitch.

In my life, there weren't that many people that I insulted, but I decided that day that I would ask forgiveness from them. They were mainly old girlfriends that I hurt in some way during my lifetime. In the next few weeks I made the calls and needless to say that they were stunned to hear my apologies.

    Just calling to say I was sorry that our relationship was only based on sex.
    You never knew the real me.
    I am surprised that I called too. Again, I'm sorry.
    Have a nice life. Bye.

Spreading the word about Career Volunteering and being humbled by the good work that Career Volunteers do has also been very gratifying. While working part-time from my college apartment for Charlie, I realized that I still needed an edge on my resume. So I joined Alpha Phi Omega co-ed, national service fraternity and knew volunteering was the answer. Meeting new people was fun, but I wasn't satisfied with group volunteering all the time. I wanted something more personal and intimate with my volunteer experiences. As I approached the United Way in my college town. Fred, the United Way Director, was quite shocked that a student came to him. He said that I was the first college student in many, many years to trek to his office. He explained that he almost always has to come to campus to ask for volunteers. I asked Fred what I could do and he suggested that my service fraternity volunteers should capitalize on the United Way's annual fund drive. I asked our fraternity's vice president of service if she could ask for United Way volunteers during our weekly meeting. However, she must have been mad that I took the initiative to seek opportunities for our fraternity because she made a poor attempt during her request at our weekly meeting. In a bitchy tone, she said, "Nobody here wants to fundraise for the United Way do they?" Of course no one volunteered. Teed off, I went back to Fred and told him that I didn't recruit anybody. He said that it was a good try, but I wasn't satisfied with just trying. I asked him, "What if I recruit just a few business majors so they may fundraise, and put the practical experience on their resume?" Fred said that would be wonderful. So I identified all the business majors from the fraternity's member list and asked them if they'd like real world experience, resume experience and references before they graduate. **(I accidentally started the first Project Sledgehammer group. See the rules in Chapter Eight.)** Six students said yes, and we raised $300 in two weeks... I happened to be walking through the Oak Grove in the middle of campus when the idea struck that this "Career Oriented Service" could apply to all majors. It certainly was a fresh twist on volunteerism. Hastily, I segmented the same list, and matched majors to local, staff hungry United Way Agencies in town. Within a few weeks, I developed a brochure and placed 1/3 of the Fraternity into Career Oriented Service volunteer positions, now known as Career Volunteering. Later, a friend of mine, Lori, a sophomore psychology major, received formal training from a local crisis intervention center, and successfully counseled a suicide call-in. She saved another person's life. That was one hell of a life changing experience for me, and was my finding moment to make Career Volunteering my life's work.

Writing this book and recording an abridged version of this book on mp3 and CD at ProjectSledgehammer.org have also been valuable life-changing experiences for me. I was lucky. I had a mentor and internship. I also had a Career Volunteering internship while marketing Career Volunteering on campus. My friend Jon Linden, owner of a mediating business, made a nice remark about me, saying, "You are 'relentless' in a very low key way, which is a rather rare combination in a 'marketing' person. Relentlessness is pretty common, but not in combination with being low key. I suspect it is one of the secrets of your success in that regard."

Amazingly, many students major in minor things. In other words, they dabble in several majors or activities on campus or during the summer and eventually find that what they're involved with lacks purpose. If you are reading this book, chances are that your life does not feel totally empty. Nevertheless, I am sure that you know others whose main objective is to only "hang out." Before I knew what I wanted to do in life, I was one of those people who wanted to play all the time. I was a little nuts, and was bored easily.

(WARNING: Following excerpts feature STUPID, DIM-WITTED stunts performed by the author while in HIS stupid, late, teen years. Accordingly, the author must insist that no one attempt to recreate or reenact any stunt performed in this book.) Regrettably though, I began to drive and enjoyed the almost unlimited freedom. In order to buy gas for my adventures, I worked a minimum wage job at a family restaurant. There happened to be an endless supply of party balloons at this restaurant, so a friend of mine and I blew up hundreds of them, stuffed them in my car, left the hatchback unlocked, and zoomed down a major highway that led into Pittsburgh, PA. We reached maximum speed and let the hatch fly open, and quickly turned around on the next exit to see our idiotic deed. We unknowingly released the balloons at the crest of a small rise, and as we sped back on the opposite side of the highway, lights from oncoming traffic illuminated the varied colors of balloons like a disco ball effect on the ground. It looked real cool, but it was a stupid thing to do. What if a car swerved because of the balloons and caused an accident? I just wasn't thinking about the consequences, like the day that I was on my friend's motorcycle. I knew how to ride, didn't have a motorcycle license, but hopped on and roared down a highway stretch with speeds in excess of 115 mph. He followed in my Camaro with a big grin on his face, according to my brother who happened to be driving the opposite direction. While I was at top speed, I hit a bump or something in the road and nearly lost my balance. Pretty stupid? Right on! Wait there's more. I played mailbox baseball. We drove on a golf course. We drove through a cornfield. We would race my Camaro against his Thunderbird. We would drive 70 mph and then slam on the brakes in the middle of the highway just to see what kind of skid marks we'd leave. On another occasion, I sat on the roof of his fast car with my legs hooked inside his sunroof while traveling at speeds in excess of 120 mph. What's more; I rode on the hood of his car traveling 60 mph, twice. The second time was not fun for my brother, who was inside screaming for my friend to slowly stop the car. I actually thought it was funny because my friend was about to turn on the windshield wipers that I was holding onto. Later, I tried to impress a friend by doing donuts in a field, only to learn that the next day in the newspaper police blotter that a dark colored sports car was spotted ruining somebody's large front lawn. Case in point, I was living my life like the MTV show, JACKASS. It wasn't funny like the show because I was putting my life in danger. I thought that I was invincible. I was living for the moment, not thinking about how my actions had consequences, and in some cases caused economic damage to other people. I was pulled over by the local and state police at least six times during high school, but somehow managed to stay out of jail. I never was caught doing this crazy stuff, but felt extremely stupid when I admitted all this to my parents when I turned 25. They asked what they did wrong while raising me. I told them that it wasn't their fault. It was a combination of testosterone, a feeling of invincibility, foolishness and not knowing what I wanted to do with my life. I was responsible for my actions, period.

    What could have happened:
    I could have won the Darwin Award if I had died.
    I died and improved the evolution of the human gene pool.
    Epitaph: He was too stupid to live.

    I look back on the stupid things that I did and want to help you avoid the same boredom that I experienced. I want to help you find your niche in life, while offering something constructive to do in the process, like Career Volunteering or starting a Project Sledgehammer group, because semesters pass

until it's too late, it's time to graduate. After graduation, instead of bouncing between majors or pointless pursuits, many of us may bounce from one job or industry to another filling the void with quick - fix wants. Looking into the future, and once our kids go off to college, we find ourselves in our 40's or 50's.
We work jobs we hate just to buy stuff we don't need.
Can you say, "Rat Race?"
"Some will sell their dreams for small desires
Or lose the race to rats
Get caught in ticking traps
And start to dream of somewhere
To relax their restless flight" 7

    I learned a valuable lesson about peer pressure when I purchased a pick-up truck that I didn't really need. I bought one because the guys that I used to hang out with all had one. However, a new car or truck is probably the worst investment because once you drive it off the lot, it severely depreciates. Not forgetting to mention that I took a four-year loan out for $609 a month, which was almost like making a mortgage payment. And I was working a job that I didn't particularly like at the time just to pay for it. I paid it off, sold it to my brother and purchased a refurbished police interceptor. That's right, I bought a used police chief's car and invested the difference. Most high school kids drive newer and fancier cars than me. However, I decided to live within and actually below my means. It is more pleasurable to see a bank account worth $30,000 while driving a used cop car rather than driving a new pick-up truck. Point is, stay out of debt so that you are more relaxed about pursuing your life's work instead of just working for a paycheck. Don't just buy some happiness. Follow your dreams instead of just following a paycheck. Sure, enjoy the finer things in life, but not frivolously, and certainly by living within your means.
    Otherwise we go into debt, are stuck working to pay the bills, and our stuff ends up owning us, and we become slaves to an empty consumer culture. Suddenly! Alarmingly! Life definition and reflection becomes priority. It may take us 40 years to start thinking about our internal world, and at that point in our lives, start asking ourselves questions like: 1) Ok, I have great kids, but what have I contributed? I think that we are evolving if we raise our kids correctly, but if you do not take care of yourself first by figuring out your life's direction, how can you be a role model for your children? 2) What definition and purpose does my life have? 3) Why isn't my life working? People between the ages of 16 and 21 are most likely are reading this book. Questions two and three are some pretty anxious uncertainties to be thinking about at these ages. However, imagine being in your forties or older asking yourself the same questions. The knee jerk reaction may be: "This is your life and it's ending one minute at a time." ibid Usually what accompanies a mid-life crisis is an urgency to preserve your youth. Advertisers make billions preying upon these troubled people. Thinking on your internal world, a good friend of mine, Joe Martin says, "It doesn't matter where you start in life, what counts is where you decide to finish." Martin Luther King, Jr. said, "If a man is called to be a street sweeper,

he should sweep streets even as Michelangelo painted, or Beethoven composed music, or Shakespeare wrote poetry. He should sweep streets so well that all the hosts of heaven and earth will pause to say, here lived a great street sweeper who did his job well." I doubt your life's calling is to be a street sweeper, but Dr. King's quote is definitely a useful statement about pride.

When was the last time that you felt proud about something constructive that you did? Now imagine having nothing to feel proud about for the rest of your life because you are stuck in a business, job or industry that you hate. And you better find a profession that you enjoy and are passionate about before you enter the workforce because most professions entail repetitive, monotonous work. Whether you work for yourself or someone else, there are tasks that require your timeliness and attention to detail, and it is hard to switch professions when you're trapped in something that you don't like, especially if you are in debt. It's difficult to switch gears and switch careers.

Don't enter into a profession for the wrong reasons. One of the primary wrong reasons is monetary greed. Don't solely want to accumulate wealth. Do what you enjoy and the money will come. For example, would you seriously want a doctor to treat your cancer if you knew that the only reason she or he went into medicine was to make money? Why would you want to enter into an industry that you don't like only to make lots of cash? See... hollow victory. Some people work all of their lives just to save up for retirement, and only really start living after retirement. Why wait to enjoy life until your retire when your body is deteriorating? Find a profession or start a business that you love. I SAY, find a hobby you love, make it your profession and never really retire!

Prevent a mid-life crisis.
If you like what you're doing, the money will come.
Ordinary people can do extraordinary things.

Briefly returning to the subject of greed, Gordon Gecko from the film WALL STREET declared, "Greed--for the lack of a better word--is good. Greed is right. Greed works. Greed clarifies, cuts through, and captures the essence of the evolutionary spirit. Greed--in all of its forms--greed for life, for money, for love, and for knowledge has marked the upward surge of mankind and greed--you mark my words—will...save...that other malfunctioning corporation called the USA." Possessing greed only to acquire excessive material wealth may end up corrupting and destroying you. However, greed can be a powerful ally to find out what you really want to do in life, and can drive you forward faster and farther than you can ever imagine. Make your life's work what you are passionate about because it's a bonus making money if you like what you're doing!

Not finding your way also comes down to a lack of initiative. Do we really take the initiative on a consistent basis? Think about it, we were born into the world as risk takers. As children our only fears were those of falling and loud noises. When you raise children, you have to literally stop them from hurting themselves. Some children leap off of furniture or steps. Kids experiment with throwing or swinging things at each other, or try wandering off to explore their environment. Kids will also say just about anything. They'll tell you if you stink, have bad breath, if you're fat, skinny, pretty, ugly, hairy and point out whatever distinctions that they observe because they are curious and fearless. Other kids are bold when talking in front of a large group. For example, my five year old was going through his first school bus orientation. During the question and answer portion at the end of the presentation, my three year old burst out that he had a question that made everybody laugh. It's been reported that adults fear public speaking more than they fear death... Isn't that interesting? Conversely, children have not been indoctrinated into society and culture, and are confident to do what they feel like. As adults, when do we lose our childlike curiosity? When did we learn to be so frightened to speak in front of a group of people? When have we lost our childlike curiosity to do things that we want to in life, only to have our dreams shot down?

According to Dr. Adell Shele, "All of these negative and apathetic attitudes that were instilled in us for more than a decade from many of our institutions actually act against you in the working world and its social context." As children, our minds were like a blank Microsoft Word document ready for the story of our lives to be written. Everyone has a book in them. There are two choices of what the chapters in the story of our lives will contain. The chapters will be positive or negative. You can choose what you want those pages to say. However, barrages from man-made, external forces that we cannot control, affect our thinking. They are: government, school, religion, the media, terrorism, corporations, corporate culture, advertising, labor unions, peer pressure, politics, etc., not forgetting to mention War, Famine, Pestilence and Death. These external forces are some components of our culture that bear down on us and influence our perceptions. Our perceptions influence our behavior. Our behavior influences our actions. If we repeat those actions, they become habit. Bad habits are hard to break. For example, smoking is a filthy habit. Big tobacco teams up with the media to advertise. Government regulates tobacco because the sales taxes generate revenue. Movies glorify smoking. Naive kids think smoking is cool, and keep consuming. Our culture generally accepts smoking. We can individually quit, but smoking won't die out until corporations, the media and government relinquish the pleasure of making gobs of cash or until society accepts the painful truth that cigarettes truly poison our bodies.

Ever since we could talk and watch T.V., haven't we been programmed to think and live a certain way? Constant media bombardment from many commercials, radio & T.V. shows & talk shows, websites and movies exhibit exceedingly bad taste with their repeated shock value without justification...

"You know your culture from your trash
You know your plastic from your cash" 25
There is a difference between art and vulgarity.
Tune out the vulgarity. Support art with your plastic or cash.

Additionally, if biased news programs keep pounding daily deceptions into our heads as the truth, we may begin to believe it. That is why bright, achieving young adults are sometimes looked upon as misfits. The media wants you to think that being smart isn't cool because they want you to buy distractions from their advertisers. One of the best things that you can do to shield yourself from the barrage of suggestive messages is take a college advertising and communications class to understand how the powerful media influences you and sort out the messages that are truly meaningful. For example, many students graduate with unrealistic job offer expectations... Don't expect a six figure starting salary. Don't expect a posh expense account. Don't expect a company car. Don't expect to fly first class. Don't expect these perks until you've earned them. Additionally, many graduates gleefully shout, "Woo Hoo!" I don't ever have to study EVER again. They think that they've earned the privilege to stop learning just because they've graduated, and feel their days of education are behind them. Knowledge is power. Use it to your advantage. The choice is yours.

Conform or be cast out. Be cool or be cast out. 7
I will not be deceived.
I break the cycle of surrendering to man-made influence.
I can always turn off the T.V. and evolve.

Our past is a powerful internal force that affects our thinking either positively or negatively. Shouldn't we hold on to the positive experiences, and just let the negative ones go? Many people hold onto their negative bag of problems until it grows so big and full that they can never let go of their problems. This psychological term is called gunny sacking. People carry their "bad past" around with them, feel sorry for themselves, expect others to pity them and lay blame ALL too easily. They use their insecurity to create new, petty reasons to be a "victim" and try to become the center of attention. Gunny sacking is dangerous. For instance, many men and women who were abused as children become abusers themselves because they cannot let go of their past. Unfortunately, many who were abused feel it's payback time to take their rage out on their spouse or children. It's amazing that they simply cannot forgive their abuser and move on. In your heart, if you forgive someone who has done something awful to you, the very first thing that you will feel is relief. You don't have to love or even like the person that you want to forgive. Just let it go. You don't even have to tell them... Forgiveness is a gift you give yourself. I grew up in a wonderful family and I've lived a good life, but there were two incidents in my past that could've marred me. I won't repeat what happened or when. Let's just say that if I weren't forgiving, and if it had played on my mind over the years, I could have descended into an emotional downward spiral.

I chose not to become damaged goods.
I am not a useful idiot.
After a decade, I chose to confront and give forgiveness.
Redemption.

One of the best ways to help an insecure person is not to pity them, but to tell them that they are responsible for their actions and maybe suggest a responsible course of action. If you really care about them, be strong to not reassure them with your pity. You are playing into their hands if you do.

Human behavior is motivated by an internal desire to avoid PAIN, and seek PLEASURE. From my previous example, it was extremely painful for me to harbor the things that were done to me and NOT forgive. It was pleasurable to confront and forgive this person, which resulted in more pleasure in the form of relief. My earlier statement that people actually fear public speaking over death is another perfect example. I do talks in front of small and large groups of young adults. Originally, it was painful for me to speak in front of an audience, but it was more painful to me that my message wasn't getting out because I was sitting on my ass. Why should I be afraid to do something that I want to do now? In other words, it is more painful for me to know that life is just passing me by each day, with a day closer to my death without spreading my message?

"If we don't take action now
We settle for nothing later
We'll settle for nothing now
And we'll settle for nothing later" 8

Also, it was pleasurable to see my young adult audience giving good non-verbal feedback during my talk, like nodding their heads in agreement. It was too painful for my friend Joe Martin to stay in the ghetto, as another example. He was EXTREMELY motivated to leave that pain behind. Whichever desire is greater will affect your course of action. Usually pain is more motivating. Additionally, Dr. Shele asserts that we have to start and continue to risk connecting with our world. Won't it be more painful if we don't?

Chapter Two: A Lesson On Initiative And Focus.

Leader to Leader Institute's Peter Drucker said, "To start with the question, 'What should I contribute?' gives freedom. It gives freedom, because it gives responsibility." And from Dr. Nathaniel Branden of Harvard University, "If I can't wait for a miracle or for someone else to do something, then what can I do; and if I choose to do nothing, to accept the status quo, am I willing to take responsibility for that decision?"

Well, with Dr. Branden's question in mind, and during a subsequent chapter in this book, I will introduce you to something clever, flexible, useful and local that you can do that offers you a long lasting benefit. It also offers an opportunity at being responsible. I don't want to be just a motivational speaker that offers only an inspirational message. I am offering an experience with a tangible end result. Career Volunteering is fulfilling and virtuous. Once you start it, you probably won't miss watching less T.V. and miss other distractions in life because you're doing something REAL.

Legendary General Robert E. Lee once said, "If habits of self-control and self-denial have been acquired during education, the great object has been accomplished." J. Steven Wilkins on Robert E. Lee says, "Fully interpreted, Lee's 'duty' is the means whereby freedom preserves itself by acknowledging responsibility. Man, then, perfects himself by discipline, and at the heart of discipline lies self-denial." These are strange concepts to us today because after all, our celebrity driven, instant gratification age encourages excessive self-indulgence without sacrifice! Even after 9/11/01, celebrities are still valued above and more respected than the everyday heroes like firemen, EMT's, police officers, nurses, doctors and soldiers who engage in quiet glory while serving and protecting us while we sleep. It still bothers me that some celebrities have been wearing FDNY or NYPD hats or shirts while blatantly promoting themselves? By associating with the real "hero" symbolism of New York's finest policemen and firemen, they transferred an aura of heroism to themselves for shameless self-promotion.

You can say, "Callous."
You can say, "Heartless."
You can say, "Obscure."
You can say, "Disgraceful."

Can our lives really be so mundane that we obsess over a celebrity's daily existence on reality T.V.? Are we foolishly taking our freedom for granted? Has the United States become just a vast playground of the world? What's unbelievable to me is people would rather watch the lives of ordinary people on reality T.V. instead of living out their own lives. While gaming with the Sims Online might be a fun way to develop new social skills, will you really have a chance to use them in your everyday life when you're spending all of your time online? Also, many of us fawn over female pop music stars. Frankly, they are promoted like porn stars. Pop music marketing executives realize that most of their female pop performers don't really have a positive message and have to mix pop music with porn type imagery to sell sugarcoated, bubble gum music. Some of their songs are fun, but isn't their imagery really degrading to women? The day I realized this was when I decided not to view women solely as sex objects. There is a difference between beauty and smut. When lust is pounded into our heads and hormones are raging, how can we resist? I can resist anything...but temptation.

Why not resist and deny yourself? There are too many distractions in life that lead us away from what is really important. What I have in mind for you in later chapters involves actual participation in REAL human interaction. I hope that you able to rid yourself of some of life's distractions in order to land your dream job and create a successful future. Yes, absolutely enjoy our way of life, our stadium games, fantasy sports, concerts, parties, shopping, chat rooms, clubs, fraternities, sororities, gossip, style and tabloid magazines, T.V., online gaming, electronic gadgets and other entertainment, but do not be distracted to the point of unbridled self-indulgence. I'll admit that I get caught up living vicariously through my sports heroes while rooting for the Pittsburgh Steelers or for Tiger Woods. Don't get me wrong, sports we watch or stories that we read opens up our imagination, but we shouldn't be obsessed enough to worship these false celebrity idols. Aren't we just paying for these celebrities to fulfill their dreams at our expense? During a weekend party, wouldn't it actually be nice to have something interesting to say about yourself? Wouldn't it be great to engage in fascinating conversation that doesn't include some sort of pop culture entertainment? Most guys my age that I'm acquainted with know more about sports statistics than the political forces that truly affect their lives.

"Some are born to move the world
To live their fantasies
But most of us just dream about
The things we'd like to be." 11
You can say, "the deliberate dumbing down of america." 24
You can say, "Socialization, not learning." ibid

Many people don't even know what political issues that their federal, state and local representatives support. Senator Gracchus from the film GLADIATOR said, "Rome is the mob. He [Caesar] will conjure magic for them and they will be distracted. And he will take their lives. And he will take their freedom. And still they will roar. The beating heart of Rome isn't the marble of the Senate. It's the sand of the Coliseum. He will give them death. And they will love him for it." History tells us that overindulgence was a ruin of the Roman Empire. Interestingly, Independence Institute's Dave Kopel wrote, "The United States has become dangerously like the degenerate Roman Republic in its final decades: a prosperous and powerful empire whose citizens and leaders are losing the virtue which is essential to the survival of a free society." Be vigilant by participating in local, state and federal government and political affairs so that your freedom is not taken away. Likewise, Career Volunteer to make your community stronger.

Choose now what you want focus on for the rest of your life because according to Earl Nightingale, "You become what you think about." And from Anthony Robbins, "As you think so you become... If you focus on something, you'll experience it." For example, I FOCUS on balancing my family life with writing this book. I make sure to do stuff with my boys, like recently taking them to see a decommissioned Army M60 tank. And I generally focus on writing into wee hours of the night while everybody is asleep. Additionally, we've all heard the expression, "You are what you eat." Well, your mind becomes what you feed it too. If you put enough good things into your mind, eventually good things will have to start coming out. If you constantly visualize that you are successful in your endeavor, you will program yourself to expect success. Athletes like Tiger Woods picture a 300-yard drive down the middle of the fairway, or visualize draining an 18-foot putt before the clubface ever touches the ball. Other golfers use different stimuli to get themselves into this hypnotic state to achieve better performance. During their back swing, they imagine the perfect sound of hitting the golf ball square with their titanium driver. Still, others may feel the solid impact of crushing a 300-yard drive in their head while addressing the ball.

To recap, use visualizations, sounds and/or feeling three to suggest maximum performance to yourself. Your possibilities are limitless by applying one or a combination of the three sensations for heightened suggestibility and receptiveness. Personally, I use both the visual and audio signals in my mind. I VISUALIZE myself as brave, courageous, calm, happy, relaxed, satisfied, stable, and wonderful on stage while delivering my message, and imagine thunderous APPLAUSE at the end. No doubt that if you FOCUS on what you're passionate about and consistently take the initiative, you'll win.

Nonetheless, DON'T focus on quick-fix wants because:
You are NOT the clothes you wear.
You are NOT the sound system you listen to.
You NOT your tattoo or pierced belly button.
You are NOT the mind-altering substances that you may have used.
You are NOT your breast implants, facelift or liposuction.
You are NOT the personalized cell phone you call from.
You are NOT reality T.V.
You are NOT a statistic in a stealth marketing campaign.
You are NOT the cigarette that you smoke.
You are NOT the car you drive!
"Don't sell your dreams for small desires." 7
Life should be about experiences, not stuff.

Hopefully through independent thought, you can determine, "What's for real and what's for sale,"23 and not be forced into buying something that you really don't need. If you can afford it, buy some excitement, but don't be suckered into an empty consumer culture. If people only live for greed and excessive materialism, they will realize on their deathbed just how hollow and empty life really was. Your belongings are just inanimate objects that can be replaced... How often have you heard people who had a close call with death or natural disasters survivors say that they are just "happy to be alive!" Survivors realize that their possessions don't define them. So get into the mind frame of a survivor, who recognizes that there is nothing more important than your good health, family & friends, and worthwhile life experiences. Focus on what you're passionate about and consistently take the initiative... If you do that you'll win.

Chapter Three: A Lesson On Contributing.

I know it's almost impossible for one person to change the world, but we can individually change our own world's right where we are with Career Volunteering, and if enough of us come together and get started, we can make our communities stronger. Career Volunteer in a group too... See Chapter Eight. Contribute now and for the rest of your life because what goes around comes around.

Good things will come around for those who Career Volunteer. These Career Volunteering success stories are organized by category:

AIDS Awareness.
"I have gone to area elementary schools to share my knowledge of AIDS with little kids and answered questions they had."
- Kelly M. (Education major teaching AIDS Awareness.)

Animal Care.
"Currently volunteering at the Hawaiian Human Society for sheltered animals and The Honolulu Zoological Society."
- Shellie K. (Pre-vet major providing time and expertise at an animal hospital.)

Community Care Work with the Elderly.
"I have been volunteering for 3 weeks now and I really like being able to meet and help people in the community. I have 7 clients who are over 55 and are low income. I like meeting new people especially seniors because they are so knowledgeable and I always learn something new about life."
- Rene A. (Community collaborative studies major assisting low income seniors.)

Computer Technical Support Volunteering.
"I really enjoy volunteering at Protonic.com. I can put my skills to use, help people, learn, gain experience for future paid jobs, and have fun doing it. I really enjoy the automatic mentor and quality assurance aspect. As an initial technician, all emails are reviewed by quality assurance and bounced back to you if you need to add to or modify your message. It is a nice learning experience."
- Brant G.

Computer Literacy.
"My volunteer experience was life changing. I have never experienced anything like it. You go in thinking that it isn't going to be any fun and you come out a different person. I would encourage everyone to volunteer at least once in their life. "
- Nikesha J. (Education Major that taught computer literacy to the computer illiterate.)
"I have had classes in computers. I have visited a nursery home and have helped out in a daycare. I love working with people."
- Molly M. (Computer science major enthused about teaching computer literacy.)
"In short, I've volunteered my time to my major field of study. I have tutored students at my University in my major, and have consulted with professors on both course and personal issues in computers."
- Rod H. (Computer science major tutoring struggling students about computers.)

"I participated in the Youth Computer Literacy Program here at Vanderbilt last spring. Our purpose was to expose younger students who probably have little access to computers elsewhere. I was paired with a young girl who was exceptionally bright but was virtually ignored at home. She loved working on the computer and always hated to leave at the end of our weekly session. It was a wonderful yet saddening experience; we taught these children something valuable and made some wonderful friendships, yet I sometimes wonder how these children will turn out... will they be successful? Some of them are so bright but no one cares for them."
- Carolyn G. (Computer science major teaching low income elementary school students basic computer literacy.)

"After several low-wage jobs, I decided to go back to school. I am enlightened by improving myself through education and feel good about giving back any skills that I learn to the community."
- Jesse M. (Computer information systems major teaching computer literacy.)

Counseling.
"While receiving formal training from a local crisis intervention center, I successfully counseled a suicide call-in. I saved another person's life."
- Lori S. (Psychology major counseling at a hot-line center.)

"I am currently a peer counselor. I will be a peer advisor during the summer program. I have also volunteered at a nursing home and a hospital."
- Chandra M. (A psychology major doing counseling work.)

"I like to talk with people about their problems. People have always been able to talk with me. I am a person that listens well and can always relate to the person I am talking with. I have been through a lot and love to help out people who are going through what I once did."
- Heather S. (Psychology major counseling at orphanages.)

Drug Awareness.
"I have had many problems involving substance abuse with myself, and it was a great opportunity to help others with what I learned from my problems and from the classroom."
- Jennifer L. (Psychology major crusading drug prevention education.)

Environmental Conservation and Preservation.
"I learned a lot of helpful information that I am sure will be of great importance, not only in my life, but in the future as well."
-Lesley D. (Environmental science major preserving a wetlands.)

"Three years ago I began doing volunteer work for a nature preservation center. I do farm work and some office work. I love it! Over the past three years I have met many people who share similar interests with me and I also got experience in areas of my interest. Now I know what I want to do with my life."
- Alyson R. (Earth science major finding her career path.)

Food Distribution to the Needy.
"I worked at the Red Cross Distribution Center."
- Neily M. (Dietetic major distributing food and supplies with The American Red Cross.)

Homelessness.
"Have worked as nurse-assistant in both long-term and home health aid facilities; have volunteered time to feed the homeless with a church organization."
-Brandy D. (Environmental and occupational health major caring for the hungry and needy.)
"Enlightening and rewarding."
- Emily J. (Inter-disciplinary studies student devoting time to help homeless and promote AIDS Awareness.)

Hospital Care Work.
"It wasn't what I had planned to be doing there, but the important thing to be - is flexible! I learned valuable skills that ended up helping me in school and employment."
- Michael L. (Psychology major as a hospital volunteer.)
"I work at Women's and Children's Hospital. I see 11 and 13 year olds go home with babies in their arms. Yet, they don't know what to do with them when they get home. I hope to be able to open the eyes of the young and keep some of them out of my hospital. Maybe I'll be able to give some of the kids their childhood. I see so many that lose it because they get pregnant. If I could show them or explain that they can't go to the mall on Sunday with their friends because they have to feed their child and nobody else but mommy can take care of them. Maybe they will think twice about having unprotected sex. This will also bring them in on AIDS awareness. This is very vital to the teenage world. If we get more of them to use condoms, then we can help eliminate the AIDS virus."
- Nedra G. (Biology major providing teen pregnancy and AIDS prevention.)
"I volunteered at a local hospital - I passed out surveys about meal plans, helped patients fill out their menu and listened as a dietician interviewed patients."
- Marie M. (Food services major recounting her food experience at a hospital.)
"When I became a volunteer at my local hospital, I decided to work in the ER unit. I love medicine, and thought this was a great opportunity where I could learn a lot of medical terminology and procedures as I worked with direct contact with the doctors. Unfortunately, I was treated like dirt and became the R.N.'s lackey. I cleaned and made beds, stamped and shredded paper, delivered charts, and transported patients to their designated rooms. The doctors were too busy, and when there was no "crap" work to do, I was always in the way. I worked my butt-off and wasted a lot of time volunteering 10+ hours for a day to make and clean beds. FINALLY, though, I got my chance. A chance set out by two people who gave me a smile and hope in my purpose for staying those extra long hours in the ER. They are the only people that actually let me do certain medical things with one special thing. They gave me respect. I put on a heart monitor on some patients, open and lay out tools and sutures for the surgical doctor, cleaned a "bloody" patient, and taught me how to put on an EKG (though I couldn't perform it because of hospital policies... I'm not certified.) I finally learned something of use in the medical field. along the way though, I never took notice of how much help I was providing. Though I disdain what I call crap work, I never knew it eased off some of the work of these R.N.'s. The ER is very busy at times so I'm sure I was of much help that I can provide. I also found out that the hospital wasn't just medical procedures, but also a relationship between the patients. Once I talked with an elderly man for 2 hours and gave a crying child a lollipop. I brought a smile to each of their faces and gave a smile to myself. I also realized I am very lucky to be at the hospital ER. I have witnessed the procedure of stitching among other things. Some of the R.N.'s never had such contact while they were at nursing school. Lastly, I thought what made it especially great was its

people. I was wrong because not only did I not get respected, but I got treated like crap. What made it great was that I did what I wanted to do and learned about medicine. However, I also was wrong again because the people do make a place special. I was part of the people who made the ER special to the sick and hurt patients who needed help. My service brought smiles to patients and gave the "mean" ER R.N.'s some load off."
- Jay N. (Pre-med major proclaiming his bedside manner while doing ER volunteer work.)

Laboratory Work.
"It makes me feel good when I help others out. It feels nice doing something for someone else and getting nothing in return, but a smile and thank you."
- Sharon E. (Pre-med major doing lab volunteer work.)

Music & Theater Community Entertainment.
"I have donated several hours of my time to volunteer work and community service over the years, and I feel that I have learned a lot from it. some things I have learned are that a helping hand is priceless. I have not seen the faces of some of the people that I have helped, but I am sure there were many smiles. I believe if more people were willing to donate even half of the time to helping others as I have, the world would be a friendlier, safer place.
- Tiffany C. (Music and theater major singing to forgotten elderly and three community theater productions.)

Organizing.
"Actually being President of ASD (sorority), I set it up so members of ASD could go to a Habitat for Humanity house and work on it one Saturday. I plan doing this next semester for our organization"
- Jill D. (Interior design major that managed a volunteer group for Habitat for Humanity.)

Physical Therapy.
"I have volunteered in physical therapy and it has increased my interest in the medical field for my major in Biology. I am interested in volunteering in either a medical field or an ecological field. This page has given me ideas on where to look for possible positions."
- Tammy S. (Biology major volunteering in physical therapy.)

Recreation & Tourism.
"I study Parks and Recreation with a specialization of Resort Recreation Management/Tourism. I experienced some volunteer activities and practicum helping, planning and implementing recreational events and activities. I also participated in a tour with people with disabilities to help them. These experiences gave me the pleasure of making people happy through recreation activities and trips."
- Tamiko I. (Parks & resort recreation management/tourism major implementing recreational events.)

Research.
"Worked on research project at Women's Research Institute and also volunteered at a local hospital."
- Stacy R. (Biology-genetics major lending her help for various projects.)

Social Work (Helping Families come together).
"Have volunteered at the Family Service Center documenting visitation between non-custodial and child(ren)."
- Janet K. (Sociology major helping to mend broken families.)

Special Education.
"Very positive! Enjoyed it a lot!! I definitely want to go into teaching & think that mentoring & tutoring are worthwhile activities for high school students to get involved in."
- Trish M. (Special Education Major who volunteered in a special education classroom at an elementary school.)

Special Needs People Care (Mental & Physical).
"I have volunteered a lot of my time to MR individuals. I want to continue to volunteer throughout my life. I have found it to be a great learning experience along with helping MR individuals realize how wonderful life really is."
- Kelly E. (Occupational therapy major helping mentally retarded individuals obtain life goals, and encourage recreational therapy.)

"I work one on one with a mentally and physically challenged adult in the B/CS area. It is very rewarding for both he and I."
- Josh G. (Biomedical science major working with a retarded citizen.)

"I have worked with handicapped students by helping them do fundraisers, as well as taking them to Kennywood Park for a day of fun and excitement. Planned picnics for them and banquets, anything to help them in school. Raised money to get a handicap accessible door put in at the community college. Working on the hotline at the women and children shelter."
- Ruth H. (Sociology major counseling, and caring for the disabled, women and children.)

Tutoring – Environment.
"I have taught students in biology and other natural sciences. I specialized in teaching 5th to 12th graders about micro and macro invertebrates on a boat for a non-profit organization. I have also lobbied for environmental legislation in Washington D.C."
- Jessica T. (Biology major not only tutoring biology, but lobbying for a better environment.)

Tutoring – Languages.
"I have recently returned from teaching English as a foreign language in Japan. While living there for 2 ½ years, I was virtually illiterate and hated that aspect of my stay. I vowed that I would help people in America who wanted to learn English as their second language. I met someone from Peru and am currently tutoring him 1 hour 3-4 times each week between classes. We're having a great time and I'm learning a lot about Peru."
- Paula B. (Education major tutoring English.)

Tutoring – Music.
"Teaching string classes (violin, viola, cello, bass). Purpose is to understand children in different school environment and to observe their behavior. Interacting with them helped me create a better environment for them to learn. Also, teaching these classes can help

build up the program and keep children involved with school activities which eventually keep them out of trouble."
- Brian V. (Psychology major teaching music to keep students focused on a positive outlet.)

Tutoring – Poetry.
"Working with high school students in a public high school translated textbook discussions into real life. It gave me a sharp awareness of the ways schools have changed or not changed since I was in high school. I became aware of the intricacies involved in teaching teenagers. It made me aware of my own privileges, past and present and put me in a position where I was initially very disconnected from the kids in the class. I learned how to build trust and respect and I grew to really like the students and worked hard at acknowledging their abilities. I discovered many wonderful poets and tried to let them know that they were writers and had talents. I enjoyed the experience while, at the same time, I felt frustrated. It was a real life peak at what it is like to teach in particular urban classrooms."
- Ena H. (Secondary education major volunteering at two local public high schools assisting a poet/teacher.)

Working with Children.
"It was a great experience and I learned a lot about people and how they react to different things."
- Unique L. (Early childhood development major volunteering with kid sports.)
"My experience can only be summed up by the words inspiring and fulfilling."
- E. J. Z. (Sociology major leading a children's youth group.)

Just like these Career Volunteers, please be open to the fact that something extraordinary can take place, by looking to yourself as a hero. Heroes like the first monkey's shot into space! I am Career Volunteering's first Space Monkey sacrificing myself for the greater good. I started Career Volunteering as a project, as a marketing major in college, and my Career Volunteering, resume experience helped me land project management and marketing positions during my career. I am a humbled Space Monkey seeing the good work Career Volunteers do.

Chapter Four: A Lesson On Better Questions.

Let's get clear about your life's definition. Just read and think about these six questions. They are very similar to those I learned from author Brian Tracy, and they have helped me.

Also, You must be sure that you are specific when answering these questions. You just can't say that you want to be rich and famous or that you just want to be happy. Happiness is not a destination. Happiness occurs while ENJOYING THE PROCESS on the journey toward your goals. I like to describe happiness with analogy of riding in a speedboat. You hop in the boat, untie the rope attached to the dock, fire up the engine and start away from shore. As you start heading to the island, which is your ultimate destination, you pass many buoys along the way. Some buoys are larger than others. As you keep traveling, the triangle shaped wake or wave behind you becomes larger and larger as your zoom toward the distant island. You make it or you don't. If you don't make it, you head back to the dock and choose another island until you can get there... Disembarking is the start of your journey. Your boat's speed is how you pace yourself. The buoys symbolize the small or large goals or obstacles along the way to accomplish or overcome. The island is a culmination of major professional and personal goals in your life. The wake that grows larger represents all the positive people and situations that enter your life because you are constantly focusing on your goal. Ever notice when you smile at someone, they smile back or when you enter a room feeling confident, people take notice, and you OWN that room? It's the same sensation while pursuing your personal or professional goals. Long lasting happiness doesn't come from ATTAINING your goal. It happens during the pursuit of your goals, and can be from simple pleasures. For instance, one of my goals is to be a good father. It's pleasurable to properly discipline my boys, and during the process, see it pay off when they listen and do something that I ask. Also, when they ask me play, 90% of the time, I drop whatever it is that I am doing and play. Playing with your kids is certainly one of life's enjoyable, simple pleasures.

Career Volunteering, in the scheme of things, is something larger than myself. After my family goes to bed, I am on the html editor updating ProjectSledgehammer.org, communicating with Career Volunteers, planning, organizing or writing. Writing this book has been an experience that stretched my creativity. I am bolder and more confident to do public speaking and get my message out. Additionally, I developed a visually stunning Public Service Announcement (PSA) that was filmed by Pittsburgh Filmmakers. View it at www.ProjectSledgehammer.org/psa.mpg. It's aired in 16 major U.S. cities.

If you honestly cannot think of the answers to the following life defining questions, let your subconscious mind work on them for you. Every night before going to sleep and each morning when you wake up, ask one of the questions to yourself. However, after you ask yourself these questions, immediately forget about them. Just let the questions sink into your subconscious. You'll be surprised how quickly the answers will come, and it'll come like a flash of lightning. In fact, use this technique anytime that you need an answer to difficult questions.

Life Defining Questions:

ONE. What have I always wanted to accomplish but was afraid to try? For me, I always wanted to go into business for myself and successfully market a product or service idea that would make a difference in people's lives. I wasn't quite sure how to get started, and didn't have the confidence to have a go of it by myself, so after college graduation, I didn't. Instead, I started out in the wireless industry. It was an exciting industry, and I thought that marketing wireless was more meaningful to me than other businesses because wireless phones could be useful to people in an emergency. Additionally, I developed and implemented a 21-county state police listing mail piece as a backup to 911 for customers. The aspect that a wireless phone may save someone's life was my "WIIFM" or "What's In It For Me." Ultimately helping others is my WIIFM because a lot of the time, "We don't feed the people, but we feed the machines." 17

    Become an Instrument of God's Will.
    It's better to give than receive.

After the wireless industry, I worked in a project management position, and oversaw the process flow of website designs and also acted as the liaison between operations and general managers in eleven states and twenty-nine markets. Unfortunately, my department was eliminated around April of 2001. It was a tough time being laid off. Months later, the terrible events of 9/11/01 transpired in our great country. Most everybody was uptight and nobody was hiring, and rightly so. I was laid off for approximately 14 months and most certainly would have obtained a job by autumn if it weren't for the fear and aftermath of 9/11. On the other hand, it was an interruption in my life that I should have experienced BEFORE graduating college. It gave me a chance to truly figure out what I wanted to do for the rest of my life. Looking back, I was extremely grateful for the 14 months that I had with my two young sons. Most fathers never get that time with their children. Also, I was able to start delivering motivational talks about the messages that are covered in this book.

    Find YOUR interruption before it's too late.
    Semesters pass until it's too late.
    It's time to graduate!

TWO. In my life, what gives me the greatest feeling of importance? In doing what? Helping others is very, very rewarding. Make genuinely helping others a habit with Career Volunteering before graduating because if you help others in the working world, it can be VERY profitable. Good customer service or pleasing your clients is defined as purely helping others. Satisfying your customer's needs results in a good reputation and more business. Also, being a team player in the office is simply characterized as helping others. If you help others on the team and are recognized for it, there is room for advancement in your career!

In the working world, I depict helping others as getting some "R and R." Not Rest and Relaxation, but Remembrance and Riches. I list Remembrance first because if I make my life's work what I am passionate about, it'll be a bonus making money since I like what I'm doing. I don't just want to accumulate wealth. I want to enjoy what I do, and realize that the money will come. If you excel at helping and servicing others in whatever profession or industry that you work in, you will be PAID HANDSOMELY for your service. For instance, my first job out of college was sales. I mentioned previously that I found some meaning in my job by creating the state police listing to report accidents and drunk drivers. Searching for meaning in my job resulted in a process improvement for the company and made a difference in the lives of my customers. My sales skyrocketed!

When I left the wireless industry for the online company, I soon realized that marketing web design products was fun, and that working in the Internet field was pretty cool, but at the end of the day, I felt empty. At the end of the day, I really wasn't making a difference, but the American Cancer Society Patient Services project management position that I later held allowed me to make an impact with cancer patients, cancer survivors and their families.

Currently, promoting Career Volunteering enables me to serve a nationwide audience. In many cases, helping others with Career Volunteering saves lives. Career Volunteer, Lori Soflarsky, was a sophomore and psychology major at Indiana University of Pennsylvania when she received formal training from a United Way sponsored suicide-hotline center. While manning the phones, she successfully counseled a suicide call-in and saved another person's life! At 19 years old, her individual contribution made a specific impact that will stay with her the rest of her life. She can draw upon her powerful experience for confidence during challenges throughout her life. And Lori's contribution was my finding moment to help others like you find your Career Volunteering contribution. Moreover, even if Lori were not an honors student, her Career Volunteering experience still beats out any Straight "A" student in virtually any job interview. Clearly, it is her experience that gives HER the edge!

THREE. What's most important to me about life? There is no question that my health, family and friends are most important to me. If you are not healthy, then you cannot enjoy life, PERIOD. To start a healthy lifestyle, you must introduce a positive, new activity into your life like changing the way you eat. You must repeat the activity everyday and not stray away from it. Instill in yourself that you must keep doing it, like how you have to brush your teeth after meals. Tell yourself that you WANT to do it daily, and if you do this activity consistently over three weeks, you will form a new positive habit. Develop new habits to force out old bad habits. Cut out the sugar in your diet. Start with something like drinking less soda. Eat fewer carbohydrates because carbs turn into sugar and ultimately into body fat. Eat less red meat. Drink or eat something living in the morning like orange juice or a banana. Supplement your diet with colloidal minerals (74 major trace and ultratrace minerals in liquid form) everyday. Take antioxidants like Ester C. Additionally, most people today do not sweat that releases toxins from your body. We live in a society that works in air conditioning, drives in air conditioning and resides in air conditioning. Exercise and sweat out the toxins in your body! Realistically, to keep the weight off, you must eat less, move more and make it a lifestyle.

My family is extremely important to me. My wife and I hug and kiss our kids. We read to our kids almost every night. We are very family oriented and spend lots of time with my parents and my mother-in-law. We like amusement parks, science centers, playing catch, wrestling, practicing golf, miniature golfing, going for walks on our farmland, church as a family, family and friends cookouts, family movies, train rides, shopping, swimming, riding bikes, going out to eat, Dairy Queen, building wooden train track layouts. My kids playing on their swing set, jumping on their trampoline, playing in their 6' x 6' sandbox, playing with their Legos, Hot Wheels, blocks, helping me fix things, educational computer games, reading, train and construction videos, rides on their uncle's tractor, backhoe, and bulldozer, etc.

I tell my kids that their mommy and daddy are here to keep them safe and secure. I tell them that I will defend my family with my life. I teach my kids about history. I teach my kids to respect their elders. I teach my kids not to talk back and to not interrupt while we are on the phone or conversing. I teach my kids manners. I teach my kids to respect firearms. I teach them to fight back if they are bullied. I teach them not to dominate someone who is weaker than they are. As I indicated before, my wife and I like to do family oriented activities together. When the kids are at my parents or mother-in-law's, we like to do the couple thing, and I generally make an idiot out of myself to entertain my wife. We have social and political conversations, talk about good food, travel, funny kid stories and indulge in sick or wry humor. In fact, I told my wife on our very first date that I was going to marry her to get to her Monty Python's Flying Circus BBC TV series video collection. Humor is very important in our marriage. Everyday we can find something funny to say or do to each other.

Experiencing life with my wife is very important to me. Before our kids, we traveled and had a fascination to explore natural disaster sites like the 1889 Johnstown, PA Flood location and museum. We will probably go on a storm-chasing trip in Oklahoma or Texas to chase a tornado. We've been to Hawaii and saw Kilauea erupt at the Pu'u'O'o crater and spew new lava into the ocean. I couldn't believe my eyes as brand new earth was forming right in front of me. In 1997 we drove in Hurricane Fran on the way to visit my brother in Virginia. Maybe us driving into a weakened hurricane probably wasn't the smartest thing to do, but it was pretty exhilarating. Nevertheless, my health and family & friends are the most important things to me in life.

FOUR. What could I contribute to the world if I knew I could not fail? Since I am merely a messenger for Career Volunteering, which is something larger than myself, why not set my expectations extremely high? I'm setting a lofty goal that a "Career Volunteering" resume section becomes standard for students graduating college. This means that I will be striving for corporate America and small to mid-size companies to accredit Career Volunteering as a viable means of practical experience on applicant resumes. Similarly, I am determined that colleges and universities expect a "Career Volunteering" section on their entrance applications as a meaningful extracurricular activity. Wouldn't it be wonderful if every young adult were INSPIRED to Career Volunteer and fill their lives with meaningful goals and experiences? I want to develop Project Sledgehammer, a project of Career Volunteering into something that will stick, and remain long after I'm gone from this Earth.

FIVE. Am I evolving? Evaluate your successes: When you're winning, identify what you are doing right and keep doing it. Assess your failures: When you are losing, find out what you're doing wrong and fix it.

In other words, during the pursuit of your goals, ask yourself if what you are doing is actually working. Ask yourself if you are really challenging yourself or just living comfortably and just buying yourself some happiness. In a broader sense, just question yourself. Question if your goals are contributing to your personal evolution, which results in the evolution of the human race one person at a time. Really think about this because what you do with your life and pass on to your children will echo on this earth for decades. Make your legacy powerful enough to live on for centuries!

SIX. Truly, what are my priorities in life because of the threat of terrorism? It's not a sugarcoated world anymore, and this question may really hit home with you because it serves as a qualifier of the preceding five questions. If you do not have the same answers from the previous five for this question, you must seriously re-evaluate what IS most important to you in your family life, your spiritual life, your professional life and your health.

Find out what mark you want to leave on this Earth. Keep focusing on these life-defining questions until you're clear. Also, be clear about this "You have to realize that someday you will die. Until you know that you are useless..." ibid Until you know that you can't really start living! For instance, Japanese Samurai entered battle knowing that they may die at any moment. Since these warriors trained and prepared as if they were going to face certain death, each would attack with audacious ferocity. Yes we all will die, hopefully in our sleep and of old age. Until that day, live your life by attacking the days on this Earth as if your time could be up at any moment.

> Until that day, develop a sense of urgency in your life.
> Until that day, accept personal responsibility for your actions.
> Until that day, live your life with passion!
> Until that day, identify what mistakes NOT to make.

I SAY don't focus on procrastination. Procrastination is a thief of your time, especially when you are required to do tasks that are monotonous and repetitive. Create urgency for yourself. Leverage yourself. If you have a term paper that must get done, dangle a carrot in front of yourself. Have something fun planned AFTER you complete your project work, like watching your favorite show or going shopping or gaming or whatever. It's all about leverage because if you really don't want to do something, you won't do it. While I don't have a washboard stomach yet, I'm in pretty good shape. I don't procrastinate whenever it's time for me to exercise because I think about how satisfied that I will be when I finish. A phrase to get into your head so that you do NOT procrastinate is, "Do it now!" And when you "do it," make sure the job is done right. My grandma said something to me that will stick with me forever. She said, "Do it right or don't do it." It doesn't matter if I'm doing something insignificant like washing my car or something crucial like delivering a speech to a thousand people. Do whatever the task is at hand, and do it WELL.

I SAY don't focus on worrying all the time. Worry is a sustained form of fear. Indecision from worrying all the time is a form of procrastination. We all want to make the right decision, but sometimes we don't and end up making mistakes. After all, Tyler Durden says, "Nothing is static. Everything is falling apart." I have made mistakes that I am not proud of that no one, except me, knows about. But once I made a decision and moved forward with action, the weight of worry was lifted off my shoulders. Nevertheless, if your decision doesn't feel right, don't fall back into worry. Simply stop what you're doing, re-evaluate, make another decision and switch gears.

I SAY don't focus on the trivial. In other words, don't get wrapped up in and bogged down with details. There have been many days that I should have been writing more and more pages for this book, but was caught up trying to make some sections too perfect. I took some advice from my friend Joe Martin who told me that my writing style DOESN'T have to be perfect. In fact, Joe said that it's better just to type out whatever I'm feeling at the moment because that is what my personality is truly reflecting. Don't get caught up over organizing. Additionally, don't get caught up doing unimportant things in life that are not even remotely related to your goals. Do you really want to waste time pursuing the trivial or chasing distractions? Don't be fooled or led away from what is really important in your life.

I SAY don't focus on envy. Humans are the only creatures on this earth that are aware of their own existence. Think about that for a minute. Think how many lives have been ruined from excessive "self-awareness," from the painful "feeling of discontent and resentment aroused by and in conjunction with desire for the possessions or qualities of another." 10   See... The neighbors have a Mercedes, so for that reason, we had better outdo them and buy a bigger, superior model Mercedes. Also see... "Hey, did you get a look at the one-carat diamond on her!" Also see... "Hmmmm, my house isn't as big as theirs, I better build an addition." Also see... "They were an 'overnight success.' I wish I could get rich quick, too." Also see... "Look at that great body on her. I wonder how much she spent on liposuction?" I can't bear to watch my family or friends get ahead!" Also see... "Please Lord, don't let them succeed! Also see... "They must have kissed plenty of ass to get that promotion. Ten years at my same job, and I'm hating it because I didn't get the promotion." Also see... a quick story about a colleague of mine. She and I worked part-time at a Big Boy Restaurant in high school, and I grew to know her through hours of mindless short-order food preparation. It was evident that she desired to become a doctor. She told me that she dreamt about being a doctor since she was four years old! Talk about being goal oriented! Overhearing our conversation, an older waitress took it upon herself to make my friend miserable while working there. Obviously, this waitress was envious about my friend's aspirations, and showed it. Recently, I caught up with my friend, now an M.D. Ten years after the fact, she recounted the story of the naysaying waitress. And guess who she saw still waitressing? Yes, it was the bitchy waitress. For a minute my friend experienced a flood of tormented memories, and realized that she had proved that waitress wrong by achieving her goal. Furthermore my friend told me that the waitress didn't recognize her, and instead of rubbing it in, kept quiet about her achievement. My friend was the stronger person, and her goals propelled her towards her lifelong dream. There's nothing wrong with waitressing, but on the other hand, the waitress practiced negative behavior and did not put forth an effort to become anything other than what she was ten years earlier.

Familiarity breeds contempt.
Misery loves company.
Losers are resentful. Winners make compliments.

Winners don't look at every person or situation and say, "What's in it for me?" Psychiatrist Sigmund Freud said, "'Envy need not be something ugly. Envy can include admiration and is reconcilable with the friendliest feeling for the person envied." In other words, positive people recognize others who may have superior possessions or qualities, but say, "GOOD FOR YOU," and MEAN it.

I SAY don't focus on fears of failure. People fail on their way to success. ACCEPT the fact that you will experience failure in your life whether it is large or small. And Thank The Lord that He's endowed us with a sense of humor so we can laugh at ourselves when we hit bottom. Poking fun at yourself and your failures softens the blow. Remember that failure is one step closer to success. Edison succeeded on the 100th attempt to invent the light bulb. The 99 times he tried was 99 steps closer to success. Also, if you keep your personal goals to yourself, it is most likely no one will ever know that you failed 99 times in the first place. We might be afraid of what others think if we fail. General George S. Patton declared, "Success is how high you bounce after you hit bottom." President Teddy Roosevelt noted, "It is not the critic who counts, not the man who points out how the strong man stumbled, or where the doer of deeds could have done better. The credit belongs to the man who is actually in the arena; whose face is marred by the dust and sweat and blood; who strives valiantly; who errs and comes short again and again; who knows the great enthusiasms, the great devotions and spends himself in a worthy cause; who at the best, knows in the end the triumph of high achievement, and who, at worst, if he fails, at least fails while daring greatly; so that his place shall never be with those cold and timid souls who know neither victory or defeat." Don't focus on the fear of failure from the perspective that it hinders your attempt to try. "Mourn your setbacks, but don't be overwhelmed by them. Conquer your own defeat to strengthen your spirit. Care more for the rewards of your community than for your own rewards. Won't you then be rewarded many times over even your greatest hopes and dreams?" 15   Why live a life of quiet desperation? Take chances. Start by Career Volunteering!

I SAY don't focus on being afraid to try. If you don't even try, you won't be able to fail or succeed. Don't live your life in limbo. When you make up your mind to do something, just DO it. Yoda of STAR WARS fame says, "Do or do not, there is no try." Ever ask a friend if they will show up for a party and they say that they'll try to make it? They don't come, do they? Ever ask a favor of someone only to hear them say that they'll try to help you and it falls through? Ever have to depend on a person to come through on an important task and they said that they'll try, and they drop the ball? "It's so easy not to try... Let the world go drifting by." 6

I SAY don't focus on fears of rejection. Fears of rejection may be another reason to not even try. Many times we are afraid to ask for something or do something because we assume that the answer will be a resounding NO! No one likes to be told no. As children, we were pounded with the word "no" because we needed to learn discipline. Can I have more cookies? Can I stay up and watch T.V. a little longer? Can you buy me every toy that I see advertised on T.V.? Can I see an R rated movie yet? Can I turn off the adult content filter on the Internet? Can I go to the dance wearing a thong and see thru dress? Can I throw my homework into the fireplace? Can I have a sports car? No. No. No. It's no wonder we want to think that people will want to say no to us because it's ingrained in us. Sometimes when we really want something so bad and we're refused, it's difficult to continue. Being told by someone that we CAN'T do something also drags your spirits down. Einstein once said, "Great spirits have always encountered violent opposition from mediocre minds." On the other hand, wanting to prove them wrong can be a powerful motivator to overcome the fear of rejection. Similarly, the pain of not having something or the pleasure of getting it keeps you asking, until you get a resounding YES!

I SAY don't focus on following the pack. Take a good look around your school or campus at what others are doing or at even what your friends are doing. Many young adults are lazy, self-absorbed, and have a "Here we are now, entertain us" 13 attitude. Here's an important piece of advice: do the OPPOSITE of what they are doing and separate yourself from the crowd! For example, if they cut class, go to class. If they are hung over from the night before, go to bed a little earlier. If they sleep in, wake up earlier. If they are gaming all the time, go to the library and study. If they are concerned with dressing sexy, wear loose clothing. If they spend all their time trying to get laid, abstain. If they are dependent on technological gadgets and accoutrements, deny yourself and spend some time outdoors. In other words, don't give into gratuitous self-indulgence. Deny yourself. If they don't have good hygiene, scrub yourself a little harder. If they have to work a crap job that wastes their time only to make car payments, downgrade or sell it. If they are overweight, eat less and exercise more. If they are vain and argue with their professors, ask your professors what they would suggest to become a successful student, and LISTEN. Martin Luther King, Jr. lamented, "Nothing pains some people more than having to think." So if the people around you aren't thinking, then THINK! And then get down on your knees and be thankful for lazy people because they are less competition for you. Even your small accomplishments as a self-starter will seem stellar in comparison to these people.

I SAY don't focus on not wanting to show up. When opportunity knocks, like a Career Volunteering opportunity, increase your chances of success by just SHOWING UP for it.

I SAY don't focus on fears of success. Amazingly, when some people become successful, they think that they are not worthy, begin to feel guilty about their success and engage in destructive behavior to sabotage their own accomplishments. It sounds crazy, but look at all the DEAD rock stars. Many had fame and fortune, couldn't handle it and spiraled downward into overdosing. While on your way to your idea of success, LET IT HAPPEN. Invite success into your life. Accept it. Build on it. Give yourself reasons to keep your success. For example, reinforce your confidence to become entrenched in your newly found success by helping others. After college, most people make the mistake that all of their reading and learning is behind them. Do the opposite of these lazy people, and invest in your success by promising yourself to never stop learning. Attend seminars, take classes, read books, listen to CD personal development programs. If you keep putting good things into your mind, eventually good things will have to start coming out.

I SAY don't focus on losing your balance. "You can do a lot in a lifetime if you don't burn out too fast." 18 My brother Jay told me, "Mark, all work and no play make Mark a boring boy." He's right. So I worked on the concept of knowing when to quit and find time to re-energize. For example, when my boys want me and ask me to do something with them like wrestling, building a new wooden layout, chasing them on their big wheels on my Razor Scooter, reading to them or watching SPONGE BOB, etc., it's TIME to take a break.

I SAY don't focus on dangerous, excessive self-indulgence. There are more serious distractions in life compared to what I mentioned in Chapter One. See... Excessively bad diets consisting of super sized sodas several times a day results in yellow rotted teeth. Super sized fries, fatty hamburgers and yummy instant gratification fast food snacks continually add pounds to America's already obese, inactive youth. My two boys are in pre-school and kindergarten and never in my life have I seen so many overweight young children attending their schools. Also see... Excessive sexual promiscuity may lead to a pregnancy resulting in the ruination of three lives – yours, your sexual partner and your baby. That's of course if your sexual partner doesn't disappear leaving you twisting in the wind to raise a child by yourself. Also see... Sex with indiscriminate multiple partners could be even worse because you may contract AIDS. Also see... Excessive partying and alcohol use may lead to ecstasy then to the misery of heroin. Also see... Excessive browsing of naughty pictures and anonymous chatting on the Internet could lead to sex chat and then to actual encounters that may lead to kidnapping, sexual torture and death.

I SAY don't focus on losing your dignity. Again, see what is going on around you at your school and DO THE OPPOSITE. A number of young adults are apathetic, self-absorbed, and have an "entertain us now" attitude. A lot of these people are selfish, ill mannered, and rude because they only care about themselves. Have some self-respect, be polite, be considerate, be tolerant, maintain your composure, and use common courtesy.

I SAY don't focus on making an issue out of race, class, gender, ethnicity, age, sexual orientation and people with disabilities. Achieve your dreams on your own accord.

I SAY don't focus on a lack of confidence. I SAY, own a room when you walk into it. Even if you are feeling a little depressed about something, manufacture a smile and walk with good posture and good body language. Most of the time, your smile will become infectious. Likewise, once you have more experience through Career Volunteering, the more confident you will become.

I SAY don't focus on making people feel guilty to get what we want. Using guilt in a relationship makes your love conditional. Your control can only be sustained by constantly alienating the other person. See... "If you loved me, we'd have unprotected sex." Also see..."If you loved me you'd just send me allowance so I wouldn't have to work a part-time job during the semester." If you find yourself using guilt to manipulate a friend, family member or lover, you had better understand that the relationship that you are in will eventually sour.

I SAY don't focus on taking your freedom for granted. Be thankful that you live in a free society! Be thankful that you have the freedom to Career Volunteer in your community to make a difference.

Learn from modern history because power corrupts. An undeniable truth is that, Communism, Fascism, Dictatorships, Totalitarianism and Socialism/Marxism have never worked throughout history. The elitists and appeasers who support these political systems are naive and blissfully ignorant because they cannot see the truth right in front of them - that central government economic and agricultural planning and iron fisted rule is not the embodiment of the human condition. Psychopath serial killers like Jeffrey Dahlmer, John Wayne Gacy, Eddie Gein, Albert Fish, Andrei Chikatilo, Jack the Ripper, Dr. Harold Shipman, Timothy McVeigh, Richard Ramirez, David Berkowitz, Ted Bundy and Charles Manson. Each psychopath APPALLED the general public by torturing and killing DOZENS IF NOT HUNDREDS of innocent people. Yet during the past century Communism through organized famine and mass killings has starved and murdered over one hundred million people! There are a few questions that we need to ask ourselves about Communism. Do you really want to give it a second chance? Today, where is the public OUTRAGE over the one hundred million deaths? Why didn't many of us learn about this in high school? Are we really learning from history to protect our freedom?

Soviet Union Communist Dictator, Josef Stalin (1879-1953), China Communist Dictator, Mao Tse-tung (1893-1976) and Adolph Hitler (1889 - 1945), originally was member of the National Socialist German Workers Party who turned into Germany's Genocidal Dictator, are among the most horrifying,

SOUL NUMBING and oppressive regimes that the world has ever seen during the past century. Combined, these and other brutal government regimes have exterminated over one hundred million people.

Let's examine Josef Stalin for a moment since it is just past the 50th anniversary of his death. Stalin tortured then starved or killed through organized famine, an estimated 20 million Russians for exhibiting independent thought. He kept the rest of the Soviet Union in line with "soul numbing oppression." 19 "When Josef Stalin was on his deathbed he called in two likely successors, to test which one of the two had a better knack for ruling the country. He ordered two birds to be brought in and presented one bird to each of the two candidates. The first one grabbed the bird, but was so afraid that the bird could free himself from his grip and fly away that he squeezed his hand very hard, and when he opened his palm, the bird was dead. Seeing the disapproving look on Stalin's face and being afraid to repeat his rival's mistake, the second candidate loosened his grip so much that the bird freed himself and flew away. Stalin looked at both of them scornfully. 'Bring me a bird!' he ordered. They did. Stalin took the bird by its legs and slowly, one by one; he plucked all the feathers from the birds little body. Then he opened his palm. The bird was lying there naked, shivering, and helpless. Stalin looked at him, smiled gently and said, 'You see... and he is even thankful for the human warmth coming out of my palm.' " 3   Literately, Stalin did to his own people the same as he did to that poor bird. Incidentally, Saddam Hussein, Iraq's deposed brutal dictator, idolized Stalin.

Poverty, fear and ignorance are the breeding ground for genocidal regimes that result in the "initiating or intensifying war, famine, democide or resettlement." 5   Learn from history to protect FREEDOM and our democracy so we don't keep making the same mistakes. One of the most important things that you can do is take a college economics and history course to understand why capitalism works and why socialism and communism do not.

Maximus from GLADIATOR says, "I have seen much of the rest of the world. It is cold and brutal and dark. Rome is the light!" Now replace Rome with America. You must understand that a FREE United States of America has only been around since 1776, and much of the world doesn't like Americans. Only since 1776, America has economically and socially surpassed the rest of the world that has been established for centuries. More technological inventions and advances in medicine have come from the United States. You see, when governments restrain its citizenry, there will be NO progress and its population will remain oppressed and poor. Recently, China banned search engines like Google because the Internet promotes too much free thought, and that is too dangerous for China's leaders. Also, many countries around the world have the same people and same culture, and when everybody's thinking is the same progress will be slower. The United States is a free society with a melting pot of many different people and cultures. Diversity has resulted in innovative thinking and tremendous growth. Capitalism works when it is not overburdened by taxes and when there is less government regulation. Capitalism has produced the most generous nation on the face of the Earth. Throughout history, there has been more blood spilled by American soldiers defending freedom around the world without the U.S. conquering and colonizing the country that it freed from oppressive, totalitarian regimes. Besides, which nation is always first on the scene with aid for the world's worst humanitarian and natural disasters? It's not the countries of the United Nations. It is the benevolent, free and just United States of America.

Even with its flaws, the United States of America is the greatest nation ever on Earth, Period. No other country even comes close. Be thankful that you have: 1. Your health; 2. Your freedoms backed by the U.S. Constitution; 3. A willing and capable military to protect you; 4. An abundant food supply; 5. Ample land to build on and own; 6. A decent health care system not socialized by the government; 7. Paved highways to take you around our great nation; 8. An Internet and other wonderful technologies invented in the United States; 9. Generous non-profit organizations like the United Way and its Agencies that offer free human services when life throws a curve ball at you; 10. An excellent higher educational system; 11. And be thankful that you have limitless opportunities and potential if you are willing to work for it.

Visit www.WhiteHouse.gov or www.Senate.gov or www.House.gov or www.SupremeCourtUS.gov or www.Archives.gov and take a few minutes to read YOUR U.S. Constitution and its Amendments, YOUR Bill of Rights, and OUR Declaration of Independence.

If you haven't already, take a day to be thankful and look around in your everyday life to see how good you really have it living in the United States. President John F. Kennedy had the right idea in the 1960's when he stated, "Today, we need a nation of Minutemen, citizens who are not only prepared to take arms, but citizens who regard the preservation of freedom as the basic purpose of their daily life and who are willing to consciously work and sacrifice for that freedom." Apply yourself with the FREE ENTERPRISE IDEA of Career Volunteering in your community to make it stronger and safer so that freedom endures.

I SAY don't focus on looking to the government for help all the time. Government should only be a last resort, safety net if family, friends, the community, churches or non-profits cannot help. The Preamble of the U.S. Constitution states: "We the people of the United States, in order to form a more perfect union, establish justice, insure domestic tranquility, provide for the common defense, promote the general welfare, and secure the blessings of liberty to ourselves and our posterity, do ordain and establish this Constitution for the United States of America." The Federal Government's primary purpose is to defend the United States from enemies, foreign or domestic. Another purpose of the Federal Government is to PROMOTE the general welfare of its citizens... The Federal Government's purpose is not to SUSTAIN a system of government in which the U.S. Congress derives their votes and power from creating a class of dependent people who rely on the government for handouts! Ultimately it is the responsibility of America's Youth to come together and focus on helping others and providing services in times of need, not the Government. Also, isn't it nice that while we are servicing others with Career Volunteering, that we are helping ourselves during the process?

Personally, I wasted years begging foundations and the government to fund my Non-profit. Finally, I decided not to wholly rely on government, and looked to myself to become a professional speaker. My speaking and book fees are financial means to support the non-profit, my family and myself.

Government is not the best answer.
You are the best resource... Rely on yourself.

I SAY don't focus on appeasing others all the time. On a simplified level, here's an example of an appeaser's thinking. Imagine that you are the appeaser, and that aggressive person approaches you, and punches you in the stomach as hard as he can. When you get up, he belts you again. You get up and are pummeled again, and again, and again.

You may have internal bleeding at this point.
Are you not totally furious at this point?

At this point, you want to hit back, and wind up to take a swing, but then the attacker stops you and says, "Now remember, you are an appeaser and you CANNOT hit back even to defend yourself!" At which point he strikes you again, and again, and again, until you DIE. See... Peace protesters protesting the war on terrorism. If terrorists or dictatorship regimes remain unchecked, then they will continue torturing and killing their own people. If these murderous regimes remain unchecked, they will destroy our way of life and kill as many liberated people as they can, INCLUDING the peace protesters because they are so full of hate. We MUST defend ourselves. Also see... The bully who keeps terrorizing the school until somebody stands up to him or her. Also see... Many women, even if they are beaten repeatedly, will stay with their husband, fiancé or boyfriend, for fear of being alone and afraid to leave the control of the abuser. Hopefully these women and children will have enough courage to leave him.

On Domestic Violence and abuse, my friend Tanya Brown writes, "On June 12, 1994 my life changed forever. I was awakened by screams from my oldest sister Denise. I will never forget that dreadful morning when I found out that my sister Nicole Brown Simpson had been murdered. I immediately ran to the back of the house to see my dad and asked him, 'Daddy, is it true what I heard?' The anguish that my entire family felt that day was too difficult to bear, so strong that you believed you would feel that way forever. In fact, the anguish became part of us. It is unimaginable how much life can sometimes change for the worse. When I heard that Nicole had been murdered, I never knew I could feel so many emotions at once: fear, anger, sadness, loss, anxiety, depression, tension, confusion, irritability, hopelessness, helplessness, pain and guilt.

What is really sad is that a wonderful woman, friend and sister and mother were suddenly gone. In my eyes, Nicole was the perfect person with a perfect life. I thought she had it all. My sister was an intelligent, strong and spirited woman. She was the type of woman that captivated you with her presence and beauty. She looked like an angel. She truly was a delight and we miss her dearly.

The trial was a blur, but I do remember sitting stoically in the Los Angeles Courthouse listening to the attorneys describe her tumultuous relationship with her former husband, O.J. Simpson. I was stunned because the woman that I thought had the perfect life actually endured 17 years of documented abuse. She was verbally degraded, locked in a wine cellar, pushed, shoved and beaten, and she documented it. A new term "Domestic Violence" became popular during the time of the trial. I scarcely heard about this term while studying psychology at San Diego and California State University at San Marcos. You always expect something like this to happen to someone else. After all, Nicole never showed any signs of being abused during visits to their Brentwood home. I never heard them fight or argue. Everything looked fine, and I never had the inkling that something could be terribly wrong with their relationship. It usually occurs out of site, behind closed doors, where the batterer can abuse his powerless victim and get away with it. Can you imagine what Nicole's children must have seen? They were victims also, in a sense. The point is that DOMESTIC VIOLENCE VICTIMS ARE ISOLATED. This is why it is important to educate yourself about the aspects of domestic violence before you become a victim or abuser yourself. Did you know that you could help prevent this horrid verbal and physical abuse crime by just volunteering one hour a month at a battered women's shelter or at an organization that offers prevention education? Once you are trained or educated by a Domestic Violence prevention education center, volunteer your public speaking skills at colleges, high schools, community centers, for corporations, and nearly anywhere in the community. Write or call your local, state and federal legislators to promote legislation that would benefit abuse victims who are mostly women and children. For example, I represented my sister during a demonstration on Capitol Hill in Washington D.C. And there are many Career Volunteering job descriptions listed in Chapter Ten of how you can do specific volunteer work related to your curriculum to make a difference in the fight against Domestic Violence.

If you are unable to volunteer with an organization, make a small donation, which still sends the message that you care. I was caught up in a moment of complete bliss, joy, love and compassion after I made such a donation at a women's shelter. The women and children were desperately grasping for the donated items. Our donations may not seem like a lot for us to give up, but it makes a WORLD of difference to the abuse victim refugees who have nothing but the clothes on their backs.

Wake up to the fact that Domestic Violence victims could be your mom, dad, sister, brother, teacher, neighbor, best friend or even yourself. Ask, "What am I going to do about it?" Are you going to sit and hope it goes away or hope the batterer will change? Nicole waited 17 years for the batterer to change until it was too late. There is nothing that I, nor anyone can do to bring her back. She is gone forever. Domestic Violence doesn't see differences. BEWARE! It can happen to you or someone you know and love. If it is happening, call the National Hotline Number: 800-799-SAFE." **Tanya Brown** is Co-founder of the Nicole Brown Charitable Foundation, and is a professional speaker specializing in life solution and relationship violence prevention. Tanya can be reached at www.TanyaBrown.net.

I SAY don't focus on abusing somebody who is weaker than you. I have a real problem with bullies. I told my boys that the best thing to do if you are bullied is to walk away. However, if the bully continues to hit, I say hit back twice as hard. Ayn Rand in 1966 said, "The truly and deliberately evil men are a small, very, very small minority. It is the appeaser who unleashes the evil men on mankind. It is the appeasers' intellectual abdication that invites the evil to take over. When a culture's dominant trend is geared to irrationality, the thugs win over the appeasers. When intellectual leaders fail to foster the best in the mixed, unformed vacillating character of people at large, the thugs are sure to bring out the worst. When the ablest men turn into cowards, the average men turn into brutes." Hold people accountable for their actions or you will be taken advantage of, especially if you keep appeasing an aggressor.

I SAY don't focus on blaming others for areas where we truly are responsible. See... Many violent criminals such as terrorists, murderers, rapists, spousal/partner abusers and child abusers are portrayed by their lawyers and in the media as the victims! Criminal actions are blamed or excused on a bad childhood, a bad marriage, drug or alcohol abuse or economic disparity, etc. Often, an insanity defense is used. Abraham Lincoln once said, "He reminds me of the man who murdered both his parents, and then when the sentence was about to be pronounced, pleaded for mercy on the grounds that he was an orphan." You name the excuse, and it's been used to defend these violent offenders. The victims themselves or their families are often victimized twice by the blame game.

What ever happened to personal responsibility? In the United States, our health care system is good enough that most of us don't worry about the consequences of an unhealthy lifestyle. Trial lawyers salivate over whom to blame and sue. Many frivolous lawsuits emerge to the point where our legal system has grown out of control! See... Sue the tobacco companies even after you have been warned that smoking is hazardous to your health. Also see... "I'm obese because fast food is addictive." Also see... Buy hot coffee from the fast food drive-thru. No cup holder? No problem! Put it between your legs! If it spills in your lap, you can sue (and win) because of your own stupidity! No Problem! Shift the blame on someone else! Also see... "I got flunked because my professors sucked." Also see... "I was late again for work because of heavy traffic, bad weather, my old unreliable car, or the snooze button, etc." Also see... "I didn't mean to hit my brother over the head with a chair, but pro wrestlers do it and never get hurt." Also see... "I didn't mean to jump off the roof, but a movie made me do it." Also see... "I didn't mean to get you pregnant; YOU should have used better protection." Also see... A pregnant mother continuing to smoke, abuse alcohol or drugs resulting in birth defects of her child. Also see... "My curriculum was too heavy to gain experience on my resume before I graduated." Also see... Plea bargain on illegal gun charges, but don't enforce existing gun laws like Project Exile that carries a 5-year minimum federal prison sentence for those caught with illegal guns. Let the violent offender walk, but sue the gun manufacturers. Also see... "I didn't mean to hurt anybody or set fires or destroy people's personal property; I joined the riot because I got caught up in the moment." Also see... "I never meant to drink and drive and kill someone, the alcohol impaired me."

Look, aren't you responsible for whatever that happens to you in your life? Absolutely! How about declaring, "I am responsible!" and hold yourself and others ACCOUNTABLE for their actions.

I SAY don't vote for politicians who only CRITICIZE and who don't offer solutions. I SAY don't vote for politicians who only viciously attack the opposition simply because they disagree with them. I SAY don't vote for politicians who have a philosophy of, "Do as I say, but don't do as I do." I SAY don't vote for politicians who ignore the truth and turn a blind eye to justice. These politicians write legislation that affects your life. Vote. Advocate for causes and for the non-profit organizations that you Career Volunteer with.

I SAY don't focus on frustration because it's guaranteed that our lives will be full of people and situations that are a direct reflection of our negative mental focus! Earlier I wrote the speedboat analogy about how you attract positive people into your life while speeding toward your goals. It works the other way too. For example, I doubt that anyone's childhood dreams were to grow up to be a drug dealer or a criminal, but if you focus on that kind of negative behavior like using hard drugs, you will find yourself attracting other drug users, dealers and unsavory characters into your life. And it's extremely difficult to get out of a destructive lifestyle. "Just when I thought I was out, they pull me back in!" - Al Pacino in The Godfather Part III as Michael Corleone expressing his frustration on trying to leave a life of crime.

Keep a list of ANSWERS, to the life defining questions listed at the beginning of this lesson and focus on them often because the more reasons you have to experience something, the more free energy and motivation you get from yourself! But what is the key to channeling this motivation into action? Well, there's a simple and effective goal setting guideline to help get you there. I learned this guideline from friend and wireless industry entrepreneur Dan Cronin... All you do is write a memo to yourself. Here is the basic format:

To: Mark
From: Myself
Date: Year of, Month of, or Week of
Subject: Top 6 Goals to Achieve

All we do to plan our time is list and prioritize our top 6 goals once year, and break them down into what we need to do monthly, and then what action to take weekly. Our top 6 weekly goals are the small victories to get us where we want in a month, and then in a year. Clearly define your goals. Set deadlines. List your reasons and benefits that you will obtain from reaching your goals. Pinpoint your obstacles. Identify the appropriate knowledge, like this book, that you will need to accomplish the goal. Identify the people that you'll need to approach or network with to achieve your goal. Brainstorm and list all possible ideas that lead to the best solutions, which help you reach your goal. Constantly analyze if you are on the right track. Keep thinking about and focusing on the attainment your goal. Keep your personal goals to yourself, and let your actions do the talking. 21

To succeed with deeds and not words became evident as I embarked on one last endeavor during the summer between my junior and senior year in college.

The first time that I ever flew in a plane, I jumped out of it.

That's right! My parents always drove on long, long family vacations, and I ended up stuck in the middle of the back seat sandwiched between my two big brothers. Oh yes, I was pummeled from Pennsylvania to Florida and back. I also have fond memories during the trip to Mississippi! It was a constant chorus of "Are we there yet? Are we there yet?"

Needless to say I had never flown before, and I jumped out of a perfectly good airplane at Cleveland Sport Parachuting center.

I met some friends while interning in Ohio, and asked one if he would like to go skydiving with me. We went through 6 hours of training and went up on a single engine Cessna. We were on our hands and knees, and packed like sardines in the plane, but fortunately everyone had a window view. I was so fascinated about how the plane circled to gain altitude to a half mile up that I wasn't scared to the beejuzus to make the tandem jump. The person in front of me chickened out, so the pilot made it an extra point to tell me that once I crawl out on the wing, I MUST jump or else he'll shake me off the plane! The pilot said that it is too dangerous to re-enter the plane while wearing a parachute. I decided to jump, and crawled out on the wing. My hands were clamped to the wing. My left leg was positioned on the wheel axle and my right leg dangled, ready to kick backward for momentum during my leap of faith off the plane. The pilot said, "Go." I looked at him like a deer caught in the headlights. Again, the pilot said, "GO!" I kicked out my right leg, arched my back to allow the tandem line better access to deploy the chute, free fell for a few seconds, and watched the plane disappear into a cloud. The tandem line successfully opens the chute, and I take my first look around from a half mile up. It's one of those beautiful, partly cloudy summer afternoon days when the sun's rays are piercing through the clouds. I can't stop laughing hysterically. Somehow, I had managed to follow my instructor's adjustment directions that were barked out from a huge loudspeaker on the ground below. I land using a "banana" style landing which is used with a round chute. You position your body like a banana where the balls of your feet hit the ground first, followed by your calf, your thigh, your butt, and finally landing and rolling over on your back. I chose to jump with a round chute over a square chute because I wanted to feel what paratroopers experienced. I land, get up, am bruised a little, am still laughing, and have a renewed appreciation of our fighting United States Airborne. The next day, I told my family and friends about my skydiving adventure. Privately setting and accomplishing my goal added to the natural high that I experienced for a few more weeks. If I told EVERYBODY in advance that I was going to jump, don't you think that I would have enjoyed the experience as much as I did? Besides, what would everyone have thought of me if I said that I was going to skydive, and then chickened out at the last minute? I would have most certainly set myself up for failure by exposing my plans.

It was the same situation with landing the character actor role in the Independent Feature Film: Our Lady Of Sorrow ~ a modern tale of madness and loss. View the trailer at www.OurLadyOfSorrow.com. I didn't say ANYTHING until I knew I got the part. People who seem to achieve "overnight success" are those who quietly and persistently keep their small victories or their catastrophic failures to themselves, and announce their success by producing results.

If our actions aren't producing the desired result, ask yourself questions like, "Am I evolving?" to steer you back on track. Change your approach and KEEP CHANGING your approach until it works because in the real world, winning isn't graded on a curve, and isn't based on luck. Winning happens when constant preparation meets opportunity. So take five minutes Monday morning to plan your weekly memo, and make a commitment to follow through.

Chapter Five: A Brief Lesson On Frustration.

As we move towards change, we'll face a lot of angry and painful situations that may, at first, try to hold us back. But remember that it was frustration and pain about problems in our world that caused me to create Project Sledgehammer. We experience problems like cancer and disease, violence, ignorance, etc. The threat of terrorism and war has produced a new attribute of our program. Career Volunteering can help young men and women unite to build resiliency in their communities. Young men and women may tap into their frustration and unite, instead of slipping into anxiety.

"Without pain and sacrifice we would be nothing." 1

Without pain and sacrifice we would not have our freedom.

It is this frustration that we should welcome. We can actually use it to motivate us. Frustration has consistently given me the leverage I needed to pull myself up, and has been a TRIGGER for me to do something.

Chapter Six: A Lesson On Doing Something.
Career Volunteer As HARD As You Can.

"**Why stand on** a silent platform.
Fight the war, f*ck the norm.
When ignorance reigns, life is lost.
When ignorance reigns, life is lost." 20
Career Volunteer as HARD as you can!
"Doing the right thing is often its only reward." – Rush Limbaugh

Earlier in this book, I mentioned a powerful program for you to participate with that I developed. It's called Career Volunteering. Career Volunteering is something clever, flexible and useful that you can do, and is easy to fit into your schedule. Starting your Career Volunteering strategy will help you beat out students who have higher grades so you can land your dream job, and create a successful future! After participating, you'll have a whole new outlook to create your desired future.

On a more sobering note, the media constantly reports stories of senseless violence and lives being lost. Here's your chance to contribute, help others and in many cases to actually save lives. You can help fight for your country, YOUR community.

There are not enough paid internships out there, but don't panic if you're about to graduate college. Career Volunteering results in obtaining quick experience and adds a quality achievement on your resume. By doing volunteer work in their chosen career area with Career Volunteering, college students gain real world experience, resume experience in your field and solid character references. If you have experience on your resume, you're more likely to get hired. Nothing impresses employers more than experience!

If you have friends still in high school, it is worth mentioning to them that they should Career Volunteer in order to obtain a college application edge. Colleges accept more students who have meaningful extracurricular activities and admirable character references listed on their entrance applications. Since colleges are being more selective with their applicants, don't let them get left behind.

Professionals Career Volunteer because it's another way to network. For example, if you laid off and wanting to volunteer, you may find that doing Career Volunteer work is a great way to make connections and do something to keep your mind stimulated during your job search.

I highly recommend that you Career Volunteer for 'staff hungry' established and recognized non-profits such as local United Way Agencies so that your desired experience and character references JUMP OUT on your resume! Opportunities listed in Chapter Ten are available for most curriculums and are LOCAL. In other words, describing your Career Volunteering experience with a nationally recognized organization during employment interviews gives you a competitive edge.

But, even before you're hired, find a profession or start a business that you LOVE. "Career Volunteering allows you to not only be prepared when you enter the workforce, but enables you to ask and answer the question, "Have I made the right choice?" If your answer is "no, it saves you from what could be a lifetime of frustration in a job or industry that does not meet your expectations." ibid   For example, Director/Writer of the Independent Feature Film, OUR LADY OF SORROW, Dennis Widmyer acknowledges, "You know, this is your life. You've got to spend it like you want to. You don't want to look back and say, 'I spent all those years in that office when I really wanted to be making films.' It becomes really clear once you take your first career-type job and you watch all these other people that are kind of just doing it because it's what you're supposed to do in life, they don't really have anything else that they want to be doing, but it's not what you want to do. You're watching them with something else in your head, saying, 'I want to be making films right now.' You've just got to go out and do it." 26   Another example was during my freshman year in college, I met a girl named Melanie who lived on my co-ed dorm floor. She was a sweet girl, but it was hard to maintain a conversation with her because she was very quiet and introverted. After talking a few times, I finally was able to find out what her major was. It was high school education, which requires a pretty strong personality to handle classrooms full of ill-behaved young adults. She revealed that her parents were high school teachers, so she made up her mind to follow in their footsteps. Do you think that she entered into the teaching profession for the wrong reasons, especially with her introverted personality? If I had developed the Career Volunteering concept as a freshman, I could have placed her into a Career Volunteer internship opportunity that helped tutor high school students in a classroom setting, and she might have realized that teaching wasn't what she wanted to do. I guarantee that she would have changed majors. Isn't it a shame how people choose the wrong major for the wrong reasons? "I found that this Career Volunteering exposure was often enough to allow the individual to make informed decisions about his or her life and the career path that they had chosen. In some cases, it resulted in students rethinking the career path that they had originally sought and changing their direction to be more in line with their personal perspectives and feelings." 14 "Additionally, our 'Career Volunteer' concept allows you to try your skills in the volunteer market place, which yields another significant benefit. It allows you to experience your chosen vocation in the outside world, so you can "reality test" your internal desires and skills." ibid   In other words, Career Volunteer and determine if you are in the right curriculum.

Career Volunteering is probably better than an internship in four ways. FIRST, volunteering is very rewarding, and you are volunteering smarter, not harder. Career Volunteering makes more of an impact than general type volunteering because more specific skills are utilized to help solve real problems that improves quality of life in your community. For example, a nursing major might be volunteering at a roadside clean up. However, the same nursing major could bring the message of the importance of AIDS Awareness or importance of annual mammograms to groups on campus or in the community; thus making more of an impact by saving lives instead of picking up trash. Another example is ONE business major might be volunteering at the same roadside clean up.

That same business major could utilize their marketing skills and organize a group of twenty for the same clean up that increases productivity TWENTY fold. There are tons more Career Volunteering examples listed in Chapters Seven and Ten.

SECOND, there is more flexibility with Career Volunteering compared with an internship because you volunteer when you can, according to your schedule. Non-profit organizations realize this and will work with you.

THIRD, since many needy, staff hungry not-for-profits don't have the manpower; you are likely to have some REAL responsibilities with your position. This means there's a good chance you'll get to use your creativity with this increased responsibility. Even if you are not an honors student, Career Volunteering experience still beats out any Straight "A" student in virtually any job interview. Clearly, it is this experience that gives YOU the edge! You will be respected in your community as a Career Volunteer, and can use that respect to successfully network and widen your circle of influence.

You can spend as little or as much time with it, perhaps Career Volunteer an hour a week during school or more during the summer, while extra credit or college course credits would be awarded via the discretion of your school. However, don't let the process of course credit approval get in the way of making a difference and making your community stronger. Career Volunteer as HARD as you can now!

LASTLY, you can start a Project Sledgehammer group by mentoring others in or out of your curriculum to Career Volunteer as a group. See the rules in Chapter Eight.

Einstein once commented that example is not only the best teacher; it's the only teacher. Hold yourself accountable, evolve and make yourself an example for others to emulate as a Project Sledgehammer leader to affect positive social change in your communities.

Chapters Seven, Parts A, B, C And D.: A Tutorial Offering Information On How You Can Find A Career Volunteering Opportunity By Using Your Local Phone Book And Other Resources Under Your Nose.

Chapter Seven, Part A.: A Lesson On Finding An Organization To Work For.

The BEST resources to find a career volunteering opportunity are Chapter Ten in this book AND "The Guide To Human Services" listing in your local phone book. You really don't need to search the Internet! Just PICK-UP your LOCAL phone book or flip to Chapter Ten and apply what you learned in this book about our unique brand of volunteering, "Career Volunteering." Then select an opportunity that suits you.

1) The Guide To Human Services listing in your local phone book lists not-for-profit agencies in alphabetical order where you can Career Volunteer. The categories usually are: Abuse and Assault; Adoption; Alcohol and Drug Problems; Camps; Children and Youth; Community Services; Consumer Problems; Day Care; The Disabled; Discrimination; Education and Enrichment; Family and Marriage; Food; Health; Home Health Care; Hospice; Hospitals; Hotlines; Housing; Job Problems; Language and Communication Problems; Legal Problems; Mental Health; Personal Problems; Prison Probation; Recreation and Social Activities; Senior Citizens; Sex Related Concerns; Social Action; Transportation Problems and Services; and Veterans Services. Usually many of these are local United Way Agencies.

2) The next resource is the Government Public Services listing in your phone book. It contains similar agencies but are run by our local state or federal government. This government listing is probably next to the Guide to Human Services listing.

3) Search Guidestar.org as a resource, which lists hundreds of thousands of not-for-profits.

4) Search our database at ProjectSledgehammer.org. Choose from the most complete and up-to-date Career Volunteering opportunities with national, staff hungry non-profits that have local offices. (Chapter Ten includes many of the same listings.)

5) Contact your local high school to find opportunities. If you are a high school student, work with your guidance counselor to find a Career Volunteering opportunity.

6) Look in the World Almanac's index for its "Trade Association and Society" section.

7) Contact your local Chamber Of Commerce to help place you.

8) Contact your House Of Worship.

Chapter Seven, Part B.: A Lesson On Contacting An Organization To Career Volunteer For.

Contacting an organization is easy. Simply identify yourself as a high school student, college student or working professional. Distinguish yourself by calling or stopping in person. Tell them what your curriculum or profession is, and that you would like to Career Volunteer in your chosen career area and obtain actual involved experience with your field, and gain real world experience. Ask how they might fit your service around your schedule. Treat it like a job interview for practice. Increase your chances of success by just SHOWING UP for it. Dress your best.

The organization will probably do the rest of the talking and suggest interesting opportunities, since they frequently lack manpower. Let them do the talking and make sure that you actively listen to what they are saying, and not try to think ahead about what your response will be. The non-profit organization that you Career Volunteer for will trust you and support what it is that you want to accomplish. They want to help you succeed because ultimately their success depends on your efforts.

If you are not satisfied with their offer, suggest some examples from the next section, Chapter Seven Part C., which lists Career Volunteering examples to use as back-ups during the interview.

Usually the first organization you select will accept you. If not, change your approach, KEEP changing your approach and select similar organizations to contact as if you were job hunting. Remember to ask for training and the level of responsibility you desire. Ask them to write a Career Volunteering section for your resume. Once that you are involved with your Career Volunteering opportunity, ALWAYS UNDERPROMISE AND OVERDELIVER! And remember, the few minutes you take here to make the initial phone call and interview can absolutely be a step towards positive change.

Chapter Seven, Part C.: A Lesson On Career Volunteering Examples To Suggest During Your Non-Profit Interview.
This section may be extremely useful if **cannot** find an opportunity from Chapter Ten that suits you. Look for your curriculum listed alphabetically. This is a pretty long section so feel free to skim through it. Also, email us at ProjectSledgehammer.org to suggest more Career Volunteering opportunities.

Accounting.
Help needy families or the elderly organize their finances and taxes. Also help people regain financial control through debt consolidation and credit counseling. Educate them to live within their means.

Agriculture.
Utilize your services at the county fair; help end hunger with local food banks, and other end hunger organizations; or teach others about the benefits of organic gardening and environmentally friendly pesticides.

Architecture.

Build or rehabilitate low-income housing; or construct handicapped accessible building enhancements.

Art.
Involve young adults in the fine arts; or preserve historical sites and museums with your historical society or association; or entertain the elderly in nursing homes or Veterans Administration (VA) Hospitals.

Aviation.
Assist on airlifts to natural disaster areas to set up emergency equipment and relief.

Biology.
Do national or state park environmental preservation; or help beautify the environment up through road-side, beach and oceanfront clean ups; or wage peace and help stop nuclear, chemical and biological weapons of mass destruction proliferation.

Business.
Promote Career Volunteering on campus with our downloadable poster; or use your business skills to organize groups to do roadside clean ups; or help people get off of welfare and get a job; or organize recreational league sports teams for kids to keep them off the streets; or utilize management skills to help organize disaster relief efforts; or organize groups during clothing and food drives.

Chemistry.
Do water testing for contaminants with local water clean ways projects; or join the war on drugs by educating elementary and high school students about drug awareness resistance education because you're knowledgeable about the damaging chemical reactions that drugs produce in the human body; or support specific drug bans that have been proven harmful.

Chiropractic.
Advocate proper ergonomics in the workplace to prevent work related injury; or teach classes, lead support groups, and organize events about arthritis and osteoporosis; or lecture on the benefits of good posture and proper spine alignment.

Communication.
Keep mainstream media bias in check; or partner with a Psychology Major and produce a High School or College talk radio show for kids, much like Dr. Laura's show for adults; or become a local media liaison and promote charitable events or causes on your high school and college TV station like ProjectSledgehammer.org's 30 second public service announcement. Contact us to obtain a free video copy.

Computer Science.
Teach computer and Internet literacy; or create web sites for non-profits; or work with the disabled to offer computer skills.

Criminology.
Organize crime watches; or work with your local police to organize high school students and other groups to erase graffiti as a step to take back your neighborhood; or help

battered women prevent domestic violence; or report Child Porn; or find missing kids; or champion firearm safety because upholding the Second Amendment carries personal responsibility with the 2.5 million times per year in the U.S. that simply brandishing a firearm was used to prevent a crime such as rape, muggings, domestic violence, robberies, car jackings, and attempted murder. 2; or join in on the war on drugs by educating elementary and high school students about drug awareness resistance education; or be against drunk driving and work to keep our highways sober; or petition for existing firearms laws to be enforced like the 5-year minimum federal prison sentence called Project Exile for those caught with illegal guns; or help battered women prevent domestic violence; or volunteer to help locate missing children; or organize block watches.

Dietetic.
Volunteer with your local food bank, and other end hunger organizations. Also help plan and deliver Meals on Wheels. Advocate proper nutrition for young and old alike since our health should be our first concern.

Early Development.
Volunteer with activities at a non-profit nursery school; or tutor children in math, reading, social and developmental skills.

Engineering.
Construct handicapped accessible building enhancements or build playgrounds for the children in your community.

English.
Tutor those that need reading skills; or read literature to the blind; or teach the English Language to inmates at a correctional facility; or tutor those who are preparing to take the high school equivalency GED (General Educational Development) test.

Finance.
Help needy families or the elderly organize their finances and taxes; or help people regain financial control through debt consolidation and credit counseling, and educate them to live within their means.

History.
Hold lectures about how Socialism/Marxism, Fascism, Totalitarianism and Communism have never worked throughout history, so we learn from history to protect freedom and our democracy; or get involved with national or state park environmental preservation; or tutor history to those, like inmates, who are preparing to take the high school equivalency GED (General Educational Development) test; or lecture about our Constitution.

Hotel, Restaurant and Hospitality.
Offer hospitality at a shelter, similar to how you would service patrons at a hotel or restaurant, to give the homeless dignity and respect; or motivate local restaurants to donate canned and non-perishable food to these very same shelters and soup kitchens; or help with your local Agency on Aging to prepare Meals on Wheels; or lecture on food safety and sanitation.

Interior Design.
Offer your services to decorate a shelter or soup kitchen, similar to how you would treat hotel or restaurant clients. Design the shelter or soup kitchen to look cheerful and feel warm, and offer the homeless some pride while they get back on their feet.

Journalism.
Keep mainstream media bias in check; or help promote local Non-profit or charitable activities by writing articles for newsletters and local newspapers.

Law.
Volunteer your services, "Pro-bono"; or advocate human rights; or petition for existing firearms laws be enforced like the 5 year minimum federal prison sentence called Project Exile for those caught with illegal guns; or support civil justice reform by promoting fairness and efficiency to the civil justice system through public education and legislative reform.

Law Enforcement.
Organize crime watches; or work with your local police to organize high school students and other groups to eradicate graffiti as a step to take back your neighborhood; or help battered women prevent domestic violence; or report child porn; or help find missing kids; or champion firearm safety because owning a firearm carries personal responsibility with the 2.5 million times per year in the U.S. that simply brandishing a firearm was used to prevent a crime such as rape, muggings, domestic violence, robberies, car jackings, and attempted murder. 2; or join the war on drugs by educating elementary and high school students about drug awareness resistance education; or promote the dangers of drunk driving and work to keep our highways sober; or petition for existing firearms laws be enforced like the 5 year minimum federal prison sentence called Project Exile for those caught with illegal guns; or report any suspicious activity relating to crime or terrorism; or lecture high school students on the dangers of speeding and encourage them to always "buckle –up"; or do child safety seat checks.

Marketing.
Create web sites for non-profits; or gain business experience & fundraise for a charitable organization.

Math.
Tutor math to inmates at a correctional facility; or tutor math to those who are preparing to take the high school equivalency GED (General Educational Development) test.

Meteorology.
Do tornado, severe thunderstorm, flash flood education and awareness.

Music.
Put on benefit shows to raise money for charity. You'll gain publicity by not only performing, but by helping a good cause; or become a companion to the elderly by entertaining them in nursing homes or Veterans Administration (VA) Hospitals; or book gigs at intermediate care facilities as music therapy for the mentally retarded; or involve young adults in the fine arts.

Nursing.
Administer your medical skills during blood drives; or volunteer at hospital lab; or become certified to teach CPR & First Aid; or offer AIDS and STD Awareness; or fight cancer!

Oceanography.
Do beach and oceanfront clean ups; or lecture on endangered species.

Optometry.
Educate senior citizens to test for cataracts, glaucoma and general eye health.

Pharmaceutical.
Support specific bans on drugs that have been proven harmful; or volunteer at hospital lab; or join in on the war on drugs by educating elementary and high school students about drug awareness resistance education because you're knowledgeable about the damaging chemical reactions that drugs produce in the human body.

Philosophy.
There are many distractions in life that lead us away from what is really important. As a society we need to choose what we want to focus on for the rest of our lives...Lecture about living within your means; or become a companion to our forgotten elderly or offer assistance, such as entertaining and lecturing relating to your curriculum, and assisting them with life's daily tasks.

Physical Education.
Keep kids active and off the streets by organizing sports teams; or teach people about the benefits of physical conditioning and exercise.

Physics.
Wage peace. Help stop nuclear, chemical and biological weapons of mass destruction proliferation.

Political Science.
Champion firearm safety because upholding the Second Amendment carries personal responsibility with the 2.5 million times per year in the U.S. that simply brandishing a firearm was used to prevent a crime such as rape, muggings, domestic violence, robberies, car jackings, and attempted murder. 2; or promote voter awareness; or lobby for organizations that have a commitment to family; or petition for existing firearms laws be enforced like the 5 year minimum federal prison sentence called Project Exile for those caught with illegal guns; or support civil justice reform by promoting fairness and efficiency to the civil justice system through public education and legislative reform.

Pre-med.
Organize rides for patients to the hospital; or lecture on AIDS and STD Awareness because of the dangers of permissive and unprotected sex; or become certified to teach CPR & First Aid; or help the elderly fill out medical information cards; or work on your bedside manner by becoming a companion to elderly shut ins or Veterans Administration (VA) Hospital residents.

Psychology.
Do hot-line and face-to-face counseling to help battered women prevent domestic violence; or Advocate teen pregnancy prevention; or teach basic parenting skills to teenage parents, which helps reduce their frustration level and the possibility for child abuse; or teach basic life skills to the homeless; or do drug prevention education; or choose a support group to counsel, such as family of murder victims, abused children, disaster victims, terrorism victims and those with terminal or mental illness.

Respiratory Therapy.
Educate people on the dangers of smoking and tobacco use; or promote asthma awareness; or advocate clean air policies.

Safety Sciences.
Develop a home safety plan for senior citizens; or prevent injuries by inspecting and fixing problems in homes owned by the elderly; or teach children about fire safety.

All Science Curriculums.
Ecology, Forestry, Biology, Physics, Chemistry, Meteorology, Geology, Oceanography, Agriculture, Zoology, Marine Biology, Environmental Engineering and Environmental Management: Get involved with responsible environmental research and conservation that is not engaged in junk science.

Sociology.
Advocate teen pregnancy prevention; or hot-line and face-to-face counseling to help battered women prevent domestic violence; or teach basic parenting skills to teenage parents, which helps reduce their frustration level and the possibility for child abuse; or drug prevention education; or help people get off of welfare and get a job; or Volunteer at non-profit nursery school; or teach basic life skills to the homeless; choose a support group to counsel, such as family of murder victims, abused children, disaster victims, terrorism victims and those with terminal or mental illness; or promote the dangers of drunk driving.

Speech Pathology.
Counsel children and adults with speech impairment disabilities; or volunteer with Special Olympics; or help the deaf or those with hearing and speech problems.

Special Education.
Organize programs and services to children and adults with mental retardation and related developmental disabilities. Also help their families; or read fine literature to the blind; or volunteer with Special Olympics.

Theater.
Put on benefit shows to raise money for charitable organizations. You'll gain publicity through performing while helping a worthy cause; or involve young adults in the fine arts; or become a companion to the elderly in nursing homes or Veterans Administration (VA) Hospitals and put on a production for them.

Veterinary.

Handle, clean and care for animal shelter animals; or visit senior citizen nursing homes with animals as companionship and therapy for our forgotten elderly to see some faces really brighten up.

Zoology.
Offer your volunteer services at your local zoo and animal shelters; or engage in responsible environmental conservation.

Chapter Seven, Part D.: A Lesson On Organizing Your Thoughts To Get Started.
  Here are some questions to think about… What am I thankful for? How can I Career Volunteer to get ahead, while enjoying the process? When can I get started? What can I really do here to be proud of? How can I treat others, as I would like to be treated? What makes me angry to Career Volunteer when I don't have to? My actions speak louder than words don't they? What is most important to me about my Career Volunteering opportunity? How much higher could I raise my self-confidence by helping others and uniting in my community? What have I accomplished to feel good and confident about? What have I learned from my accomplishments? How would it feel if I introduce Career Volunteering to three of my friends? What will it cost me if I don't have resume experience and real world experience after I graduate? Lastly, "Without pain and sacrifice we would be nothing," 1; am I nothing or will I evolve and contribute?

*Chapter Eight: Rules - Starting A Project Sledgehammer Group.

Perhaps you have already Career Volunteered, your project is over and you want to do more. **Become a Project Sledgehammer Leader. Mentor others in or out of your curriculum to Career Volunteer as a group.** Hold Project Sledgehammer at your school in the dorm, fraternity or sorority, wherever. Start one during the summer when you are bored. It's free to all. It will never cost to get in. We want you, not your money. You're welcome to start or join a Project Sledgehammer group.
See the Rules:
The First Rule about Project Sledgehammer is you talk about Project Sledgehammer.
The Second Rule about Project Sledgehammer is you TALK about Project Sledgehammer.1 Absolutely tell 3 of your friends about Project Sledgehammer to recruit new members.
The Third Rule about Project Sledgehammer is you must first lead by example and Career Volunteer. You must complete our survey after participating at ProjectSledgehammer.org or in the last page of this book.
The Fourth Rule about Project Sledgehammer is your group must meet at least once a month for at least a half hour. Refreshments are at your discretion. Also discretionary -- scheduling speakers such as leaders from the community, who know about real life outside the campus bubble.
Fifth Rule -- visit ProjectSledgehammer.org and submit your email and new group member emails with the title, "Project Sledgehammer Group" in the subject line.
***Sixth Rule** -- (a) if a many of you are in the same curriculum and want to Career Volunteer for one cause or organization, DO it. i.e. If a group of business majors want to fundraise for the United Way on the same Career Volunteering project for marketing experience, then DO it. (b) If students in your group have assorted curriculums, you can still work with the same cause or organization, but while gaining varying resume experience by Career Volunteering differently. i.e. 3 Career Volunteers with the United Way: a business major fundraising, a journalism major writing a human interest story for the school or local newspaper, and a communications major submitting a public service announcement to their school or local T.V. station to publicize the United Way campaign -- Enjoy the process. Do the work. Have fun in your group!
Seventh Rule -- measure your results and record your success by helping to write either sections for college applications or for a resume section or both. Utilize the resources in this book, and on ProjectSledgehammer.org.
Eighth Rule -- one person talks at a time during a Project Sledgehammer group so you may debate and collaborate in a civil manner.
Ninth Rule -- the Project Sledgehammer Rules are displayed during the meeting. Copy this rule page to display or visit ProjectSledgehammer.org for a printer friendly version of the rules or photocopy this page.
The Tenth and final Rule -- if this is your first meeting, you HAVE to listen to the Project Sledgehammer audio program or read this book afterwards.
Project Sledgehammer Group Recruiting Suggestions:
Tell three of your friends about this book or about ProjectSledgehammer.org.
Request that your favorite websites trade links with us at ProjectSledgehammer.org. Visit our "Promote Us" or "Trade Links" page on ProjectSledgehammer.org for our official banner ads and linking info. Distribute several printer friendly posters from ProjectSledgehammer.org on your campus or anywhere. Talk about Project Sledgehammer in your favorite chat rooms... Thanks.

Chapter Nine: A Call To Action

It is not the sugarcoated world that you may think it is. Blade from the vampire film, BLADE, says, "You better wake up. The world you live in is just the sugarcoated topping. There's another world beneath it, the real world, and if you want to survive in it, you'd better learn to pull the trigger!" There are worse things than vampires in our world. Everyday there is a battle against:
Cancer, AIDS, and disease -- terrorism -- nuclear, chemical and biological weapon proliferation -- Marxism/Socialism, Fascism, Communism, and Dictatorships -- war and civil war -- violent crime -- drug trafficking and drug abuse -- spousal or partner abuse -- child abuse -- drunk drivers -- racism -- illiteracy -- apathy -- low voter turnout -- high school drop outs -- teen pregnancy -- child porn -- media bias -- poverty, starvation -- natural disasters -- excess materialism and empty consumer culture, debt, etc.

I think I'm only beginning to understand all this myself, and what it means to our generation. We want to do something; however, much of the volunteer work that is offered has hardly anything to do with your curriculum. Many general skill volunteering projects offer little if no responsibility, and involve monotonous tasks like: stuffing envelopes, picking up trash, organizing clothes or supplies, simple companionship, making phone calls, etc. But think about it, don't the major issues still remain in control, leaving many of the volunteers overwhelmed like much more can be done? Shouldn't more of the volunteers' skills be utilized?

Absolutely! Volunteer SMARTER, not harder with Career Volunteering. Make more of an impact by using your skills to help solve real problems in your community!

My dad worked in a psychiatric ward in a Veteran's Hospital for 34 years. He was an occupational therapist who held the key for many patients to help rid them of their mental disease. I'm sort of following in his footsteps because Career Volunteering can be a key that unlocks your future. With your future, don't plan to fail by failing to plan. Start planning now and join other Every Day Hero Career Volunteers.

Give not your life, as MILLIONS of Americans have in the past for our freedom, but give an hour of your knowledge and skills once a week. If you feel powerless or uncertain because of the threat of terrorism, make your community stronger.

I want you to do me a favor.
I want you to Career Volunteer as HARD as you can!
If you are bored then what is your excuse for doing nothing?!

Evolve! Fill the rest of your life with meaningful goals and experiences, not excuses... Develop Career Volunteering strategies to land your dream job, and create a successful future! If you choose to join us, and our cause, I'll be personally very grateful.

After you participate, visit the last page of this book or online at ProjectSledgehammer.org to take our survey for tracking purposes. Thank you.

Chapter Ten: A Lesson On Doing Some Problem Bashing In Your Curriculum With These National And International Organizations, Such As United Way Agencies. They Are Organized By Curriculum.

LOCAL opportunities are available right where you are. Call the national or international non-profit organizations below to locate and have your call transferred to the office nearest you. Explain that you saw the ProjectSledgehammer.org opportunities and wish to Career Volunteer. Opportunities are available for most curriculums.

Search Google.com, Superpages.com or your favorite search engine if the web address or phone number is not correct. If you still can't find the correct phone number, try dialing 00 for AT&T "Double O" Info or dial your area code then 555-1212 for local directory assistance. You'll receive the current phone number for your organization to contact. In addition, if any 800 numbers we give you are incorrect, dial 800-555-1212 for Toll-Free 800 number directory assistance.

Project Sledgehammer, a project of Career Volunteering, Inc. is not affiliated with any of these organizations. However, it is highly recommended that you Career Volunteer for 'staff hungry' established and recognized non-profits like the ones listed in this chapter so that your desired experience and character references JUMP OUT on your resume! Share these opportunities with your Project Sledgehammer group! See Chapter Eight. Look for your curriculum listed alphabetically. This is a pretty long section of approved Career Volunteering opportunities, so feel free to skim to your curriculum.

National
Accounting.
IRS Volunteer Income Tax Assistance (VITA) and Tax Counseling for the Elderly (TCE) Career Volunteering Description: "The IRS is reaching out to individual taxpayers to educate and assist with tax preparation. We are able to offer taxpayers free income tax assistance during February, March, and through April 15th to the low income, disabled, elderly and non-English speaking through Volunteer Income Tax Assistance (VITA) and Description: The IRS is reaching out to individual taxpayers to educate and assist with tax preparation. We are able to offer taxpayers free income tax assistance during February, March, and through April 15th to the low income, disabled, elderly and non-English speaking through Volunteer Income Tax Assistance (VITA) and Tax Counseling for the Elderly (TCE)."
http://www.irs.gov
800-829-1040

National
Agriculture.
4H Council
Career Volunteering Description: "Acquire basic skills, explore career opportunities, and gain experience in the workplace."

http://www.fourhcouncil.edu

International
Agriculture.
Institute for International Cooperation & Development
Career Volunteering Description: "At IICD we offer program in India Africa and Central America. The programs are 6-13 months. There is a 52-5 month training period."
http://www.iicd-volunteer.org
616 782 0450

National
Architecture.
Habitat for Humanity
Career Volunteering Description: "Build or rehabilitate low-income housing. Watch the happy people move in to what you built for them."
http://www.habitat.org
(229) 924-6935

National
Architecture.
KaBOOM!
Career Volunteering Description: "Volunteer on a planning committee or a Build Day and build playgrounds that bring together different people to accomplish one goal: to create a safe, fun and challenging place for children to play with the support of their family and friends."
http://www.kaboom.org
kim@kaboom.org
202/659-0215, ext. 225

National
Architecture.
National Coalition for the Homeless
Career Volunteering Description: "Help build or fix up houses or shelters."
info@nationalhomeless.org
http://www.nationalhomeless.org
202.737.6444

National
Architecture.
National Organization on Disability
Career Volunteering Description: "Assist the construction of handicapped accessible building enhancements or sidewalk enhancements. Help build accessible playgrounds too!"
ability@nod.org
http://www.nod.org
(202) 293-5960

National.
Art.

Flock of Angels & Nicole Brown Charitable Foundation
Career Volunteering Description: "'Virtual Angels' volunteer from the comfort of their home or office. After being introduced, Angels are assigned to smaller 'Flocks' that are responsible for individual projects such as: Anti Violence Music and Art's Festival, Memorial Season, Nicole's Memorial, Live Events and more."
http://www.flockofangels.org
info@flockofangels.org
949-588-6262

National
Aviation.
Civil Air Patrol
Career Volunteering Description: "Do airlifts that aid disaster areas, do pollution indexes, and narcotic searches from the air."
http://www.capnhq.gov/
800-FLY-2338

National
Biology. - If you or someone you know has been touched by cancer, this is for you.
American Cancer Society
Career Volunteering Description: "1. Speak about American Cancer Society Early Detection guidelines through the American Cancer Society Ambassador Program to community groups, community health fairs, volunteer fairs, civic organization meetings, coalition meetings, screenings, etc. Training involved.
www.cancer.org
800.227.2345

National
Biology.
American Cetacean Society (ACS)
Career Volunteering Description: "Work to protect whales, dolphins, porpoises, and their habitats through education, conservation and research."
http://www.acsonline.org
310-548-6279

National
Biology.
Clean Beaches Council
Career Volunteering Description: "Sustain America's beaches."
http://www.cleanbeaches.org
540-373-1436

National
Biology.
Ocean Conservancy
Career Volunteering Description: "Help protect our oceans by responding to our Action Alerts."
!http://www.oceanconservancy.org
info@oceanconservancy.org
(202) 429-5609

National
Biology.
Wildlife Conservation Society
Career Volunteering Description: "Inspire care for nature, provide leadership in environmental education, and help sustain our planet's biological diversity."
http://wcs.org
718-220-5100

National
Biology.
World Wildlife Fund
Career Volunteering Description: "Save endangered species, preserve wild places, and address global threats."
http://www.worldwildlife.org
1-800-CALL-WWF

International
Business.
Aamar Nijer - My Own
Career Volunteering Description: "A solution for poverty in India's Villages is capitalism and entrepreneurship through 'Aamar Nijer Self Dependent Villages.' Develop international import and export marketing and management skills while developing a market in your college or hometown for apparel and traditional crafts from these SPIRITED villagers in India as well as Korak's independent films."
http://www.korakday.com/DirectWork.htm
korak_day@hotmail.com

National
Business.
100 Black Men of America, Inc.
Career Volunteering Description: "Serve as a strong force for overcoming the cultural and financial obstacles that have limited the achievements of African-American youth, with a particular emphasis on young African-American males."
http://www.100blackmen.org
(404) 688-5100

National
Business.
A Better Chance
Career Volunteering Description: "Help increase the number of well-educated minority youth capable of assuming positions of responsibility and leadership in American society."
http://www.abetterchance.org
(212) 456-1920

National
Business.
Alliance To Save Energy
Career Volunteering Description: "Advance the overall goal of moving the United States and the world toward a more energy-efficient, sustainable future."
http://www.ase.org/

202/857-0666

National
Business. - If you or someone you know has been touched by cancer, this is for you.
American Cancer Society
Career Volunteering Description: "1. Assist the American Cancer Society in raising money to fund research and support its mission of eliminating cancer and diminishing suffering from cancer. Delivering Daffodils to businesses and schools, forming Relay for Life Teams, attending an Auction or obtaining Auction prizes, are just a few of the Career Volunteer fundraising opportunities available.
2. Help the American Cancer Society local unit in the process of recruiting, training and retaining and recognizing volunteers to do the important work of the Society.
3. Provide clerical and customer service support to a local American Cancer Society unit. Customer service duties include: telephone inquiries, typing, mailings, filing, copying, inventory, materials ordering, stamping of literature, etc.
4. Serve on a committee to plan an American Cancer Society Survivor's Conference.
5. Become an American Cancer Society grassroots advocate or organizer and help shape public policy about cancer related matters and the rights of cancer patients at the local, state, and national levels of government."
www.cancer.org
800.227.2345

National
Business.
American Plastics Council
Career Volunteering Description: "Broadcast quality professional format tapes are available to TV stations and can be tailored for use in many communities for plastics recycling."
http://www.americanplasticscouncil.org
800-2-HELP-90

National
Business.
Best Buddies
Career Volunteering Description: "Assist individuals to locate and maintain jobs of their own choosing by providing ongoing support and training."
http://www.bestbuddies.org/
(305) 374-2233

National
Business.
Citizens Against Government Waste (CAGW)
Career Volunteering Description: "Promote CAGW's mission to eliminate waste, mismanagement, and inefficiency in the federal government."
http://www.cagw.org
membership@cagw.org
202-467-5300

National
Business.
Citizens for a Sound Economy (CSE)

Career Volunteering Description: "Get weekly news and the latest info to support free enterprise, lower taxes and limited government."
http://www.cse.org
cse@cse.org
888 JOIN CSE

National
Business.
Communities In Schools
Career Volunteering Description: "Offer technology training for the future, career counseling and employment skills, college preparation and scholarship opportunities."
http://www.cisnet.org
cis@cisnet.org
800-CIS-4KIDS

International
Business.
END WAR, INC.
Career Volunteering Description: "HELP THE LUCOM PLAN LOCATE THE ENEMY. How? Sign and convince others to sign the petition at www.EndWar.com. By the State Department, in accordance with the U.S. Counter Terrorism Law, 22 USC 2708, raising the present ineffective reward to a One-Billion-Dollar Reward for the capture of a terrorist leader or a head of state who is secretly developing weapons of mass destruction or who starts a war. No leader would start a nuclear war, conventional war or terrorist attack if he knew he was going to be hunted down and killed because of the reward."
http://www.endwar.com
peace@endwar.com

National
Business.
Goodwill Industries International, Inc.
Career Volunteering Description: "Volunteer with a business advisory councils that are involved in activities such as developing and reviewing curriculum, providing placement assistance, giving technical advice and networking with other influential members of the business community."
contactus@goodwill.org
http://www.goodwill.org
(240) 333-5200

National
Business.
National Alliance to End Homelessness
Career Volunteering Description: "Train homeless individuals for employment and help implement the Ten Year Plan to End Homelessness."
naeh@naeh.org
http://www.naeh.org
(202) 638-1526

National
Business.

National Coalition for the Homeless
Career Volunteering Description: "Train homeless individuals for employment. Also work and organize an event at a shelter."
info@nationalhomeless.org
http://www.nationalhomeless.org
202.737.6444

National
Business.
Renew America
Career Volunteering Description: "Become a part of a network of community and environmental groups, businesses, government leaders and civic activists to exchange ideas and expertise for improving the environment."
http://solstice.crest.org/environment/renew_america
202.721.1545

National
Business.
Nicole Brown Charitable Foundation
Career Volunteering Description: "CALL to PROTECT provides recycled wireless phones pre-programmed to 911 to victims of domestic violence FREE OF CHARGE. These phones serve as an emergency lifeline - one that they might not have access to otherwise. Please help the NBCF's effort to provide all victims of domestic abuse with a wireless phone."
http://www.nbcf.org
info@nbcf.org
(949) 283-5330

National
Business.
Ronald McDonald House Charities
Career Volunteering Description: "Help manage collecting new toys for visiting children at Ronald McDonald House playrooms."
http://www.rmhc.org
630.623.7048

National
Business.
Small Business Administration
Career Volunteering Description: "Help needy families or the elderly organize their finances and taxes."
http://www.sba.gov
800.827.5722

National
Business.
Ted Nugent USA Hunters for the Hungry Program
Career Volunteering Description: "Organize a hunt for hungry outing. Since 1989, this loosely knit, nationwide organization has seen more than 1 million pounds of game meat

have been collected and distributed across the country. The hunter pays the standard processing fee and food banks pick up and distribute the meat within days of its arrival."
http://www.tnugent.com
517-750-9060

National
Business.
Toys for Tots Foundation (Marines)
Career Volunteering Description: "Help collect new, unwrapped toys during October, November and December each year and manage the distribution those toys as Christmas gifts to needy children in the community in which the campaign is conducted."
http://www.toysfortots.org
(703) 640-9433

National
Business.
United Way of America
Career Volunteering Description: "Gain business experience and network while fundraising for your local United Way during its campaigns. Search for your local United Way organization on our website."
http://www.UnitedWay.org
(703) 836-7112

National
Business.
YouthBuild USA
Career Volunteering Description: "Offer job training, education, counseling, and leadership development opportunities to unemployed and out-of-school young adults, ages 16-24, through the construction and rehabilitation of affordable housing in their own communities."
http://www.youthbuild.org
ybinfo@youthbuild.org
617-623-9900

International
Business.
Loving The People
Career Volunteering Description: "We need a creative serious person interested to find new sponsors and volunteers for helping abandoned Romanian children. Visit our site."
http://www.pennyjames.btinternet.co.uk/LTP/
004059478501

National
Chemistry. - If you or someone you know has been touched by cancer, this is for you.
American Cancer Society
Career Volunteering Description: " 1. Speak at an American Cancer Society Youth Tobacco Leadership event and a local school health advisory council about the negative chemical reactions that take place in the body after smoking a cigarette or chewing spit tobacco. Involves training.

2. Speak about American Cancer Society Early Detection guidelines through the American Cancer Society Ambassador Program to community groups, community health fairs, volunteer fairs, civic organization meetings, coalition meetings, screenings, etc. Training involved."
www.cancer.org
800.227.2345

National
Chemistry.
American Plastics Council
Career Volunteering Description: "Broadcast quality professional format tapes are available to TV stations and can be tailored for use in many communities for plastics recycling."
http://www.americanplasticscouncil.org
800-2-HELP-90

National
Chemistry.
Combustion Institute
Career Volunteering Description: "Promote and disseminate research in combustion science. It's member's carry out the purpose of the Institute."
http://users.telerama.com/~combust/
412-687 1366

National
Chemistry.
World Wildlife Fund
Career Volunteering Description: "Save endangered species, preserve wild places, and address global threats."
http://www.worldwildlife.org
1-800-CALL-WWF

National
Chiropractic.
Spina Bifida Association of America
Career Volunteering Description: "Help individuals with Spina Bifida to make informed decisions about their health care choices."
http://www.sbaa.org/
(800) 621-3141

National
Communications.
Accuracy In Media
Career Volunteering Description: "Join Accuracy In Media - a non-profit, grassroots citizens watchdog of the news media that critiques botched and bungled news stories and sets the record straight on important issues that have received slanted coverage."
http://www.aim.org/
ar1@aim.org
(202) 364-4401

National

Communications. - If you or someone you know has been touched by cancer, this is for you.
American Cancer Society
Career Volunteering Description: "1. Help the American Cancer Society local unit in the process of recruiting, training and retaining and recognizing volunteers to do the important work of the Society.
2. Become an American Cancer Society grassroots advocate or communicator and help shape public policy about cancer related matters and the rights of cancer patients at the local, state, and national levels of government.
3. Serve on a committee as a media liaison with local media outlets who helps promote the American Cancer Society Relay for Life, its signature fundraising event. Involves training.
4. Serve on a committee to plan an American Cancer Society Survivor's Conference."
www.cancer.org
800.227.2345

National
Communications.
The American Muslim Council
Career Volunteering Description: "Educate to not retaliate against Muslim Americans. Muslim Americans condemn terrorist attacks as un-Islamic, barbaric, and inhumane."
http://www.amconline.org
202 789 2262

National
Communications.
American Muslim Society
Career Volunteering Description: "Educate to not retaliate against Muslim Americans. Muslim Americans condemn terrorist attacks as un-Islamic, barbaric, and inhumane."
http://www.masnet.org/
(703) 998-6525

National
Communications.
American Plastics Council
Career Volunteering Description: "Broadcast quality professional format tapes are available to TV stations and can be tailored for use in many communities for plastics recycling."
http://www.americanplasticscouncil.org
800-2-HELP-90

National
Communications.
Citizens Against Government Waste (CAGW)
Career Volunteering Description: "Promote CAGW's mission to eliminate waste, mismanagement, and inefficiency in the federal government."
http://www.cagw.org
membership@cagw.org
202-467-5300

National
Communications.

Citizens for a Sound Economy(CSE)
Career Volunteering Description: Get weekly news and the latest info to support free enterprise, lower taxes and limited government."
http://www.cse.org
cse@cse.org
888 JOIN CSE

National
Communications.
Communities In Schools
Career Volunteering Description: "Offer technology training for the future, career counseling and employment skills, college preparation and scholarship opportunities."
http://www.cisnet.org
cis@cisnet.org
800-CIS-4KIDS

National
Communications.
Electronic Privacy Information Center(EPIC)
Career Volunteering Description: "Privacy is a fundamental human right. Protect personal privacy. Protect electronic privacy."
http://www.epic.org/
202 483 1140

International
Communications.
END WAR, INC.
Career Volunteering Description: "HELP THE LUCOM PLAN LOCATE THE ENEMY. How? Sign and convince others to sign the petition at www.EndWar.com. By the State Department, in accordance with the U.S. Counter Terrorism Law, 22 USC 2708, raising the present ineffective reward to a One-Billion-Dollar Reward for the capture of a terrorist leader or a head of state who is secretly developing weapons of mass destruction or who starts a war. No leader would start a nuclear war, conventional war or terrorist attack if he knew he was going to be hunted down and killed because of the reward."
http://www.endwar.com
peace@endwar.com

National
Communications.
FRS (Foundation for Rural Service)
Career Volunteering Description: "Educate the public on rural telecommunications issues and advocates on behalf of the industry in order to improve the quality of life throughout rural America."
http://www.frs.org
703/351.2026

National
Communications.
Media Research Center

Career Volunteering Description: "The Media Research Center is the nation's largest media watchdog. Help bring political balance to the nation's news media and responsibility to the entertainment media."
http://www.mediaresearch.org/
(703) 683-9733

National
Communications.
Nicole Brown Charitable Foundation
Career Volunteering Description: "'CALL to PROTECT provides recycled wireless phones pre-programmed to 911 to victims of domestic violence FREE OF CHARGE. These phones serve as an emergency lifeline - one that they might not have access to otherwise. Please help the NBCF's effort to provide all victims of domestic abuse with a wireless phone."
http://www.nbcf.org
info@nbcf.org
(949) 283-5330

International
Communications.
Face to Face International
Career Volunteering Description: "1. Face to Face is seeking translators of English and the languages of our partner organizations for various volunteer projects. Languages needed: Danish, Dutch, Finnish, Flemish, French, German, Italian, Norwegian, Portuguese, Spanish, and Swedish.
2. Face to Face is seeking volunteers with library or archives experience to organize our collections. Library or archives experience is essential.
3. Face to Face is seeking volunteers with video production or distribution experience to execute a video distribution project. Experience with video distribution is preferred."
http://www.facetoface.org
212-809-6539

National.
Communications.
Flock of Angels & Nicole Brown Charitable Foundation
Career Volunteering Description: "'Virtual Angels' volunteer from the comfort of their home or office. After being introduced, Angels are assigned to smaller 'Flocks' that are responsible for individual projects such as: Web Research, Proof Reading, Anti Violence Music and Art's Festival, Memorial Season, Nicole's Memorial, Anti Violence Newsletter, Live Events and more."
http://www.flockofangels.org
info@flockofangels.org
949-588-6262

International
Communications.
One World One People for Peace
Career Volunteering Description: "Be an international contributing journalist or author. Contribute a positive article that inspires humanitarian work or reflects the peaceful spirit of the One World One People for Peace home page message and mission statement."

http://www.1world1people.org
articles@1world1people.org

National
Computer Science. - If you or someone you know has been touched by cancer, this is for you.
American Cancer Society
Career Volunteering Description: " Demo www.cancer.org to assisted living facilities and those senior citizens who are not Internet literate."
www.cancer.org
800.227.2345

National
Computer Science.
Communities In Schools
Career Volunteering Description: "Offer technology training for the future, career counseling and employment skills, college preparation and scholarship opportunities."
http://www.cisnet.org
cis@cisnet.org
800-CIS-4KIDS

National
Computer Science.
Flock of Angels & Nicole Brown Charitable Foundation
Career Volunteering Description: "'Virtual Angels' volunteer from the comfort of their home or office. After being introduced, Angels are assigned to smaller 'Flocks' that are responsible for individual projects such as Web Research, Proof Reading, Nicole's Memorial, Anti Violence Newsletter, Live Events and more."
http://www.flockofangels.org
info@flockofangels.org
949-588-6262

National
Computer Science.
Hugs for Health Foundation
Career Volunteering Description: "Hugs for Health offers the opportunity to express creativity by assisting with the on-going development of the Foundation's website."
http://www.hugs4health.org
JoD@hugs4health.org
562-594-0663

National
Computer Science.
National Multiple Sclerosis Society
Career Volunteering Description: "At the National Multiple Sclerosis Society we offer may varied volunteer opportunities, i.e., website management, public relations activities, office and special event support."
http://www.nmss.org
800-344-4867

National

Computer Science.
Welfare To Work
Career Volunteering Description: "Help retrain some of America's workforce that desperately needs application skills to be computer literate."
http://wtw.doleta.gov/

National
Computer Science.
YouthBuild USA
Career Volunteering Description: "Offer job training, education, counseling, and leadership development opportunities to unemployed and out-of-school young adults, ages 16-24, through the construction and rehabilitation of affordable housing in their own communities."
http://www.youthbuild.org
ybinfo@youthbuild.org
617-623-9900

National
Cosmetology. - If you or someone you know has been touched by cancer, this is for you.
American Cancer Society
Career Volunteering Description: "Distribute American Cancer Society Look Good, Feel Better brochures to hair salons, wig salons or prosthesis stores in your area. Set meetings to play the powerful video that describes the camaraderie that women experience while learning beauty techniques to combat the appearance related side effects of cancer treatment. This is a great way to network with salons."
www.cancer.org
800.227.2345

National
Cosmetology.
Locks of Love
Career Volunteering Description: "Cut your family or friends' hair to donate, and get involved to provide hairpieces to financially disadvantaged children under the age of eighteen with medical hair loss."
http://www.locksoflove.org
info@locksoflove.org
88?-896-1588

National
Cosmetology.
Wigs for Kids
Career Volunteering Description: "Get involved and help provide hair replacement solutions for children affected by hair loss due to chemotherapy, alopecia, burns and other medical conditions. Cut your friends or family's hair to donate."
440.333.4433
http://www.wigsforkids.org
info@wigsforkids.org

National
Criminology.
Citizen Corps - Federal Emergency Management Agency

Career Volunteering Description: "Help individuals prepare themselves and their families for disasters in the Citizen Corps."
http://www.citizencorps.gov
(202) 566-1600

International
Criminology.
END WAR, INC.
Career Volunteering Description: "HELP THE LUCOM PLAN LOCATE THE ENEMY. How? Sign and convince others to sign the petition at www.EndWar.com. By the State Department, in accordance with the U.S. Counter Terrorism Law, 22 USC 2708, raising the present ineffective reward to a One-Billion-Dollar Reward for the capture of a terrorist leader or a head of state who is secretly developing weapons of mass destruction or who starts a war. No leader would start a nuclear war, conventional war or terrorist attack if he knew he was going to be hunted down and killed because of the reward."
http://www.endwar.com
peace@endwar.com

National
Criminology.
National Crime Prevention Council
Career Volunteering Description: "Learn to protect yourself, secure your home and property, safeguard your family and safeguard your school. Help create communities where children can be children and people once isolated by crime and fear can enjoy being a part of a thriving neighborhood."
webmaster@ncpc.org
http://www.ncpc.org
(202) 466-6272

National
Criminology.
National Domestic Violence Hotline
Career Volunteering Description: "Promote 1-800-799-SAFE(7233) to help women get help through crisis intervention, and help battered women through crisis intervention and become a Volunteer Hotline Advocate."
512-453-8117
http://www.ndvh.org

National
Criminology.
Nicole Brown Charitable Foundation
Career Volunteering Description: "Educate yourself about the aspects of domestic violence before joining the force to shield yourself from ignorant senior officers."
http://www.nbcf.org
info@nbcf.org
(949) 283-5330

National
Criminology.
NRA

Career Volunteering Description: "Self-defense is a basic human right. Work at the local, state, and federal levels to defend our Second Amendment rights. Champion firearm safety because upholding the Second Amendment carries personal responsibility with the 2.5 million times per year in the U.S. that simply brandishing a firearm was used to prevent a crime such as rape, muggings, domestic violence, robberies, car jackings, and attempted murder. 2 Petition for existing firearms laws be enforced like the 5-year minimum federal prison sentence called Project Exile for those caught with illegal guns."
http://www.nra.org
800-NRA-3888

National
Criminology.
Pink Pistols
Career Volunteering Description: "Armed Gays don't get bashed. Dedicate yourself to the legal, safe, and responsible use of firearms for self-defense of the sexual-minority community. Pink Pistols no longer believes it is the right of those who hate and fear gay, lesbian, bi, trans, or polyandrous persons to use us as targets for their rage. Self-defense is our RIGHT."
www.PinkPistols.org
admin@pinkpistols.org
(617) 686-2564

National
Criminology.
Second Amendment Sisters
Career Volunteering Description: "Self-defense is a basic human right. Women: work at the local, state, and federal levels to defend our Second Amendment rights. 'More guns less crime means that States with the largest increases in gun ownership also have the largest drops in violent crimes.' 12"
http://www.sas-aim.org
(877) 271-6216

National
Criminology.
Street Safe Kids
Career Volunteering Description: "Help kids stay safe. Encourage community action. Promote safety awareness. Recognize differences in people. Reduce reasons for violence. Resolve conflict for good of all. Help protect property values in the process."
http://www.compeace.org
compeace@concentric.net
510-530-1319

National
Dental. - If you or someone you know has been touched by cancer, this is for you.
American Cancer Society
Career Volunteering Description: "Speak at an American Cancer Society Youth Tobacco Leadership event and a local school health advisory council about the negative effects of spit tobacco and smoking. Involves training."
www.cancer.org
800.227.2345

National
Dietetic.
4-H Council
Career Volunteering Description: "Acquire basic skills, explore career opportunities, and gain experience in the workplace."
http://www.fourhcouncil.edu

National
Dietetic. - If you or someone you know has been touched by cancer, this is for you.
American Cancer Society
Career Volunteering Description: "1. Speak about Prevention via American Cancer Society nutrition guidelines and/or Patient Services nutrition modules through the American Cancer Society Ambassador Program to community groups, community health fairs, volunteer fairs, civic organization meetings, coalition meetings, screenings, etc. Training involved.
2. Individuals can help the American Cancer Society advocate for Comprehensive School Health Education to develop school health advisory councils in their local school districts. Involves training."
www.cancer.org
800.227.2345

National
Dietetic.
Catholic Charities USA
Career Volunteering Description: "Support families with a better nutrition plan."
http://www.catholiccharitiesinfo.org
(703) 549-1390

National
Dietetic.
Family Violence Prevention Fund
Career Volunteering Description: "Educate the nation about the needs of children and encourage preventive investment through better nutrition before children get sick."
http://www.endabuse.org
(415) 252-8900

National
Dietetic.
Ronald McDonald House Charities
Career Volunteering Description: "Help keep a stocked kitchen of nutritious canned goods and non-perishables for visiting families of the Ronald McDonald Houses. Contact your local House to set up a donation or to get suggestions for a shopping list."
http://www.rmhc.org
630.623.7048

National
Dietetic.
Share Our Strength

Career Volunteering Description: "Apply your knowledge with Share Our Strength and help plan meals for the needy."
http://www.strength.org/
800.969.4767

National and International
Dietetic.
CARE (Cooperative for Assistance and Relief Everywhere)
Career Volunteering Description: "Work with poor communities to find lasting solutions to poverty. Help the world's poor with enough food to eat and clean water to drink, having access to health care, basic education and economic opportunity, and having the ability to participate in decisions affecting one's family and community."
info@care.org
http://www.care.org
404-681-2552

International
Dietetic.
International Food Information Council
Career Volunteering Description: "Teach proper nutrition because our health should be our first concern."
http://www.ific.org

National
Dietetic.
Ted Nugent USA Hunters for the Hungry Program
Career Volunteering Description: "Hunt for nutritious protein for the needy. Since 1989, this loosely knit, nationwide organization has seen more than 1 million pounds of game meat have been collected and distributed across the country. The hunter pays the standard processing fee and food banks pick up and distribute the meat within days of its arrival."
http://www.tnugent.com
517-750-9060

National
Early Childhood Development.
A Better Chance
Career Volunteering Description: "Help increase the number of well-educated minority youth capable of assuming positions of responsibility and leadership in American society."
http://www.abetterchance.org
(212) 456-1920

National
Early Childhood Development. - If you or someone you know has been touched by cancer, this is for you.
American Cancer Society
Career Volunteering Description: "Individuals can help the American Cancer Society advocate for Comprehensive School Health Education to develop school health advisory councils in their local school districts. Involves training."
www.cancer.org

800.227.2345

National and International
Early Childhood Development.
CARE (Cooperative for Assistance and Relief Everywhere)
Career Volunteering Description: "Work with poor communities to find lasting solutions to poverty. Help the world's poor with enough food to eat and clean water to drink, having access to health care, basic education and economic opportunity, and having the ability to participate in decisions affecting one's family and community."
info@care.org
http://www.care.org
404-681-2552

National
Early Childhood Development.
Child Welfare League of America
Career Volunteering Description: "Invest time in our children, our future."
http://www.cwla.org
(202) 638-2952

National
Early Childhood Development.
Communities In Schools
Career Volunteering Description: "Work with a child as a tutor or mentor, and help with after-school and extended-hours programs."
http://www.cisnet.org
cis@cisnet.org
800-CIS-4KIDS

National
Early Childhood Development.
Family Violence Prevention Fund
Career Volunteering Description: "Educate the nation about the needs of children and encourage preventive investment before children get sick or into trouble, drop out of school, or suffer family breakdown."
http://www.endabuse.org
(415) 252-8900

National
Early Childhood Development.
Lutheran Services In America
Career Volunteering Description: "Offer a wide spectrum of human services to children."
http://www.lutheranservices.org
800-664-3848

National
Early Childhood Development.
National Coalition for the Homeless

Career Volunteering Description: "Find out if there are children who could benefit from tutors or mentors."
info@nationalhomeless.org
http://www.nationalhomeless.org
202.737.6444

National
Early Childhood Development.
NRA
Career Volunteering Description: "Teach accident avoidance with the Eddie Eagle gun safety program. If children find a firearm lying out unsupervised, they will learn to: STOP! Don't Touch. Leave the Area. Tell an Adult."
http://www.nra.org
800-NRA-3888

National
Ecology.
American Cetacean Society (ACS)
Career Volunteering Description: "Work to protect whales, dolphins, porpoises, and their habitats through education, conservation and research."
http://www.acsonline.org
310-548-6279

National
Ecology.
Nat'l' Audubon Society
Career Volunteering Description: "Help identify ways to protect birds, other wildlife and the environment with the new Administration and the new Congress."
http://www.audubon.org
(212) 979 3000

National
Ecology.
Ocean Conservancy
Career Volunteering Description: "Help protect our oceans by responding to our Action Alerts!"
http://www.oceanconservancy.org
info@oceanconservancy.org
(202) 429-5609

National
Ecology.
Wildlife Conservation Society
Career Volunteering Description: "Inspire care for nature, provide leadership in environmental education, and help sustain our planet's biological diversity."
http://wcs.org
718-220-5100

National

Ecology.
World Wildlife Fund
Career Volunteering Description: "Save endangered species, preserve wild places, and address global threats."
http://www.worldwildlife.org
1-800-CALL-WWF

National and International
Economics.
CARE (Cooperative for Assistance and Relief Everywhere)
Career Volunteering Description: "Work with poor communities to find lasting solutions to poverty. Help the world's poor to have access to economic opportunity, and having the ability to participate in decisions affecting one's family and community."
info@care.org
http://www.care.org
404-681-2552

National
Economics.
Catholic Charities USA
Career Volunteering Description: "Reduce poverty, support families and empower communities."
http://www.catholiccharitiesinfo.org
(703) 549-1390

National
Economics.
Citizens for a Sound Economy(CSE)
Career Volunteering Description: "Get weekly news and the latest info to support free enterprise, lower taxes and limited government."
http://www.cse.org
cse@cse.org
888 JOIN CSE

National
Economics.
National Council on Economic Education
Career Volunteering Description: "Promote economic literacy. Help others develop the real-life skills they need to succeed: to be able to think and choose responsibly as consumers, savers, investors, citizens, members of the workforce, and effective participants in a global economy."
http://www.nationalcouncil.org/
800-338-1192

National
Education.
A Better Chance

Career Volunteering Description: "Help increase the number of well-educated minority youth capable of assuming positions of responsibility with their finances in American society."
http://www.abetterchance.org
(212) 456-1920

National
Education.
CARE (Cooperative for Assistance and Relief Everywhere)
Career Volunteering Description: "Work with poor communities to find lasting solutions to poverty. Help the world's poor with enough food to eat and clean water to drink, having access to health care, basic education and economic opportunity, and having the ability to participate in decisions affecting one's family and community."
info@care.org
http://www.care.org
404-681-2552

National
Education.
Catholic Charities USA
Career Volunteering Description: "Reduce poverty, support families and empower communities."
http://www.catholiccharitiesinfo.org
(703) 549-1390

National
Education.
Communities In Schools
Career Volunteering Description: "1. Work with a child as a tutor or mentor, and help with after-school and extended-hours programs.
2. Offer technology training for the future, career counseling and employment skills, college preparation and scholarship opportunities."
http://www.cisnet.org
cis@cisnet.org
800-CIS-4KIDS

International
Education.
END WAR, INC.
Career Volunteering Description: "HELP THE LUCOM PLAN LOCATE THE ENEMY. How? Sign and convince others to sign the petition at www.EndWar.com. By the State Department, in accordance with the U.S. Counter Terrorism Law, 22 USC 2708, raising the present ineffective reward to a One-Billion-Dollar Reward for the capture of a terrorist leader or a head of state who is secretly developing weapons of mass destruction or who starts a war. No leader would start a nuclear war, conventional war or terrorist attack if he knew he was going to be hunted down and killed because of the reward."
http://www.endwar.com
peace@endwar.com

National

Education.
Family Violence Prevention Fund
Career Volunteering Description: "Educate the nation about the needs of children and encourage preventive investment before children get sick or into trouble, drop out of school, or suffer family breakdown."
http://www.endabuse.org
(415) 252-8900

National
Education.
Lutheran Services In America
Career Volunteering Description: "Offer a wide spectrum of human services to children and families, to older people and to people with disabilities."
http://www.lutheranservices.org
800-664-3848

National
Education.
National Alliance to End Homelessness
Career Volunteering Description: "Train homeless individuals for employment and help implement the Ten Year Plan to End Homelessness."
naeh@naeh.org
http://www.naeh.org
(202) 638-1526

National
Education.
National Coalition for the Homeless
Career Volunteering Description: "1. Find out if there are children who could benefit from tutors or mentors.
2. Train homeless individuals for employment."
info@nationalhomeless.org
http://www.nationalhomeless.org
202.737.6444

National
Education.
NRA
Career Volunteering Description: "Teach accident avoidance with the Eddie Eagle gun safety program. If children find a firearm lying out unsupervised, they will learn to: STOP! Don't Touch. Leave the Area. Tell an Adult."
http://www.nra.org
800-NRA-3888

National.
Education.
Nicole Brown Charitable Foundation
Career Volunteering Description: "Educate yourself about the aspects of domestic violence before joining the classroom to shield yourself from ignorant senior teachers and

administrators. Also volunteer your public speaking skills at colleges, high schools, community centers, for corporations, and virtually anywhere in the community."
http://www.nbcf.org
info@nbcf.org
(949) 283-5330

National and International
Education.
ProLiteracy Worldwide
Career Volunteering Description: "Teach the illiterate to read."
http://www.proliteracy.org
info@proliteracy.org
888-528-2224

National
Education.
YouthBuild USA
Career Volunteering Description: "Offer counseling and leadership development opportunities to unemployed and out-of-school young adults, ages 16-24, through the construction and rehabilitation of affordable housing in their own communities."
http://www.youthbuild.org
ybinfo@youthbuild.org
617-623-9900

National
Engineering, Civil.
Association for Bridge Construction and Design Pittsburgh Chapter
Career Volunteering Description: "a) Educate bridge designers, constructors, federal, state, and local officials, as well as the general public in the vital role of safe bridges in our society. b) Improve and encourage the science of bridge design, and construction."
http://www.abcdpittsburgh.org/
(412) 392-8793

National and International
Engineering, Civil.
CARE (Cooperative for Assistance and Relief Everywhere)
Career Volunteering Description: "Work with poor communities to find lasting solutions to poverty and infrastructure. Help the world's poor with enough clean water to drink."
info@care.org
http://www.care.org
404-681-2552

National
Engineering, Civil.
Citizen Corps - Federal Emergency Management Agency
Career Volunteering Description: "Help individuals prepare themselves and their families for disasters in the Citizen Corps."
http://www.citizencorps.gov
(202) 566-1600

National
Engineering, Civil.
Habitat for Humanity
Career Volunteering Description: "Build or rehabilitate low-income housing. Watch the happy people move in to what you built for them."
http://www.habitat.org
(229) 924-6935

National
Engineering, Civil.
KaBOOM!
Career Volunteering Description: "Volunteer on a planning committee or a Build Day and build playgrounds that bring together different people to accomplish one goal: to create a safe, fun and challenging place for children to play with the support of their family and friends."
http://www.kaboom.org
kim@kaboom.org
202/659-0215, ext. 225

National
Engineering, Civil.
National Coalition for the Homeless
Career Volunteering Description: "Help build or fix up houses or shelters."
info@nationalhomeless.org
http://www.nationalhomeless.org
202.737.6444

National
Engineering, Electrical.
Alliance To Save Energy
Career Volunteering Description: "Advance the overall goal of moving the United States and the world toward a more energy-efficient, sustainable future."
http://www.ase.org/
202/857-0666

National and International
Engineering, Environmental.
CARE (Cooperative for Assistance and Relief Everywhere)
Career Volunteering Description: "Work with poor communities to find lasting solutions to poverty and infrastructure. Help the world's poor with enough clean water to drink."
info@care.org
http://www.care.org
404-681-2552

National
Engineering, Environmental.
Combustion Institute
Career Volunteering Description: "Promote and disseminate research in combustion science. Its members carry out the purpose of the Institute."

http://users.telerama.com/~combust/
412-687 1366

National
Engineering, Environmental.
Federal Emergency Management Agency
Career Volunteering Description: "Help individuals prepare themselves and their families for tornados, hurricanes, severe thunderstorms, flash floods, blizzards and other natural disasters."
http://www.fema.gov
(202) 566-1600

National
Engineering, Environmental.
Ocean Conservancy
Career Volunteering Description: "Help protect our oceans by responding to our Action Alerts!"
http://www.oceanconservancy.org
info@oceanconservancy.org
(202) 429-5609

National
Engineering, Environmental.
World Wildlife Fund
Career Volunteering Description: "Save endangered species, preserve wild places, and address global threats."
http://www.worldwildlife.org
1-800-CALL-WWF

International
Engineering, Mechanical.
ASM INTERNATIONAL
Career Volunteering Description: "ASM fosters the understanding and application of engineered materials and their research, design, reliable manufacture, use and economic and social benefits. This is accomplished via a unique global information-sharing network."
http://www.asmchapters.org/pittsburgh/
(724) 226- -6383

National and International
Engineering, Mechanical.
CARE (Cooperative for Assistance and Relief Everywhere)
Career Volunteering Description: "Work with poor communities to find lasting solutions to poverty and infrastructure. Help the world's poor with enough clean water to drink."
info@care.org
http://www.care.org
404-681-2552

National

Engineering, Mechanical.
KaBOOM!
Career Volunteering Description: "Volunteer on a planning committee or a Build Day and build playgrounds that bring together different people to accomplish one goal: to create a safe, fun and challenging place for children to play with the support of their family and friends."
http://www.kaboom.org
kim@kaboom.org
202/659-0215, ext. 225

National
English.
Communities In Schools
Career Volunteering Description: "Work with a child as a tutor or mentor, and help with after-school and extended-hours programs."
http://www.cisnet.org
cis@cisnet.org
800-CIS-4KIDS

National.
English.
Flock of Angels & Nicole Brown Charitable Foundation
Career Volunteering Description: "'Virtual Angels" volunteer from the comfort of their home or office. After being introduced, Angels are assigned to smaller 'Flocks' that are responsible for individual projects such as Web Research, Proof Reading, Anti Violence Newsletter, Nicole's Memorial and more."
http://www.flockofangels.org
info@flockofangels.org
949-588-6262

National and International
English.
ProLiteracy Worldwide
Career Volunteering Description: "Teach the illiterate to read."
http://www.proliteracy.org
info@proliteracy.org
888-528-2224

National
English.
National Coalition for the Homeless
Career Volunteering Description: "Find out if there are children who could benefit from tutors or mentors."
info@nationalhomeless.org
http://www.nationalhomeless.org
202.737.6444

National
English.

National Multiple Sclerosis Society
Career Volunteering Description: "Recruit elementary and middle school students throughout the country to participate once again in the MS READaTHON, which raises money to end the devastating effects of MS."
http://www.nmss.org

National
English.
Radio Information Service
Career Volunteering Description: "Read to those who are Blind, or have Cerebral Palsy, Muscular Dystrophy, severe dyslexia on Pittsburgh, PA based Radio Information Service, which refers volunteers to radio stations across the country."
http://www.readingservice.org
(412) 488-3944

International
Film.
Aamar Nijer - My Own Productions
Career Volunteering Description: "A solution for poverty in India's Villages is capitalism and entrepreneurship through 'Aamar Nijer Self Dependent Villages.' This is an opportunity to market and support Korak's independent films. As the films earn money, profits go to India for poor children, their schools, helpless women, unemployed poor people and all the various projects taken up by the production company of this film."
http://www.korakday.com/MyKarma.htm
korak_day@hotmail.com

National
Finance.
Catholic Charities USA
Career Volunteering Description: "Reduce poverty, support families in their financial planning and empower communities."
http://www.catholiccharitiesinfo.org
(703) 549-1390

National
Finance.
A Better Chance
Career Volunteering Description: "Help increase the number of well-educated minority youth capable of assuming positions of responsibility with their finances in American society."
http://www.abetterchance.org
(212) 456-1920

National and International
Finance.
CARE (Cooperative for Assistance and Relief Everywhere)
Career Volunteering Description: "Work with poor communities to find lasting solutions to poverty. Help the world's poor with economic opportunity, and having the ability to participate in decisions affecting one's family and community."
info@care.org

http://www.care.org
404-681-2552

National
Finance.
Citizens for a Sound Economy(CSE)
Career Volunteering Description: "Get weekly news and the latest info to support free enterprise, lower taxes and limited government."
http://www.cse.org
cse@cse.org
888 JOIN CSE

National
Finance.
IRS Volunteer Income Tax Assistance (VITA) and Tax Counseling for the Elderly (TCE)
Career Volunteering Description: "The IRS is reaching out to individual taxpayers to educate and assist with tax preparation. We are able to offer taxpayers free income tax assistance during February, March, and through April 15th to the low income, disabled, elderly and non-English speaking through Volunteer Income Tax Assistance (VITA) and Description: The IRS is reaching out to individual taxpayers to educate and assist with tax preparation. We are able to offer taxpayers free income tax assistance during February, March, and through April 15th to the low income, disabled, elderly and non-English speaking through Volunteer Income Tax Assistance (VITA) and Tax Counseling for the Elderly (TCE)."
http://www.irs.gov
800-829-1040

National
Forestry.
Environmental Defense Fund
Career Volunteering Description: "Reduce pollution through activism."
http://www.environmentaldefense.org
800-684-3322

National
Forestry.
National Audubon Society
Career Volunteering Description: "Help identify ways to protect birds, other wildlife and the environment with the new Administration and the new Congress."
http://www.audubon.org
(212) 979 3000

National
Forestry.
World Wildlife Fund
Career Volunteering Description: "Save endangered species, preserve wild places, and address global threats."
http://www.worldwildlife.org
1-800-CALL-WWF

National
Foreign Languages.
Accuracy In Media
Career Volunteering Description: "Join Accuracy In Media. We are looking for volunteers who would like to translate AIM's website into other languages."
http://www.aim.org/
ar1@aim.org
(202) 364-4401

International
Foreign Languages.
Face to Face International
Career Volunteering Description: "Face to Face is seeking translators of English and the languages of our partner organizations for various volunteer projects. Languages needed: Danish, Dutch, Finnish, Flemish, French, German, Italian, Norwegian, Portuguese, Spanish, and Swedish."
http://www.facetoface.org
212-809-6539

National
Geology.
Alliance To Save Energy
Career Volunteering Description: "Advance the overall goal of moving the United States and the world toward a more energy-efficient, sustainable future."
http://www.ase.org/
202/857-0666

National
History. - If you or someone you know has been touched by cancer, this is for you.
American Cancer Society
Career Volunteering Description: "Speak about the unique history of the American Cancer Society and the timeline of cancer through the Ambassador Program to community groups, community health fairs, volunteer fairs, civic organization meetings, coalition meetings, screenings, etc. Training involved."
www.cancer.org
800.227.2345

National
History.
Civil War Preservation Trust
Career Volunteering Description: "Learn as you help preserve civil war battlefields, ultimately preserving the central event in the life of our nation."
http://www.civilwar.org
202.367.1861

National
History.
Communities In Schools

Career Volunteering Description: "Work with a child as a tutor or mentor, and help with after-school and extended-hours programs."
http://www.cisnet.org
cis@cisnet.org
800-CIS-4KIDS

National
Hotel, Restaurant and Hospitality.
National Coalition for the Homeless
Career Volunteering Description: "Incorporating your skills to aid in efforts of housing first programs or supportive housing programs."
http://www.nationalhomeless.org
info@nationalhomeless.org
202.737.6444

National
Journalism.
Accuracy In Media
Career Volunteering Description: "Join Accuracy In Media - a non-profit, grassroots citizens watchdog of the news media that critiques botched and bungled news stories and sets the record straight on important issues that have received slanted coverage."
http://www.aim.org/
ar1@aim.org
(202) 364-4401

National
Journalism. - If you or someone you know has been touched by cancer, this is for you.
American Cancer Society
Career Volunteering Description: "Serve on a committee as a media liaison with local media outlets who helps promote the American Cancer Society Relay for Life, its signature fundraising event. Involves training."
www.cancer.org
800.227.2345

National
Journalism.
American Muslim Council
Career Volunteering Description: "Educate to not retaliate against Muslim Americans. Muslim Americans condemn terrorist attacks as un-Islamic, barbaric, and inhumane."
http://www.amconline.org
202 789 2262

National
Journalism.
American Plastics Council
Career Volunteering Description: "Broadcast quality professional format tapes are available to TV stations and can be tailored for use in many communities for plastics recycling."
http://www.americanplasticscouncil.org
800-2-HELP-90

National
Journalism.
Citizens Against Government Waste (CAGW)
Career Volunteering Description: "Report the latest news on campus on how Washington is wasting your money, and action alerts so that you can take part in urgent tax and spending battles."
http://www.cagw.org
membership@cagw.org
202-467-5300

National.
Journalism.
Flock of Angels & Nicole Brown Charitable Foundation
Career Volunteering Description: " 'Virtual Angels' volunteer from the comfort of their home or office. After being introduced, Angels are assigned to smaller 'Flocks' that are responsible for individual projects such as: Web Research, Proof Reading, Anti Violence Music and Art's Festival, Memorial Season, Nicole's Memorial, Anti Violence Newsletter, Live Events and more."
http://www.flockofangels.org
info@flockofangels.org
949-588-6262

National
Journalism.
Media Research Center
Career Volunteering Description: "The Media Research Center is the nation's largest media watchdog. Help bring political balance to the nation's news media and responsibility to the entertainment media."
http://www.mediaresearch.org/
(703) 683-9733

National
Journalism.
Radio Information Service
Career Volunteering Description: "Broadcast to those who are Blind, or have Cerebral Palsy, Muscular Dystrophy, severe dyslexia on Pittsburgh, PA based Radio Information Service which refers volunteers to radio stations across the country."
http://www.readingservice.org
(412) 488-3944

International
Journalism.
Loving The People
Career Volunteering Description: "We are interested to find a person who would like to develop our social work program in order to make it more and more efficient for the help of the abandoned children."
http://www.pennyjames.btinternet.co.uk/LTP/
004059478501

International
Journalism.
One World One People for Peace
Career Volunteering Description: "Be an international contributing journalist or author. Contribute a positive article that inspires humanitarian work or reflects the peaceful spirit of the One World One People for Peace home page message and mission statement."
http://www.1world1people.org
articles@1world1people.org

National
Journalism.
Ted Nugent USA Hunters for the Hungry Program
Career Volunteering Description: "Report on and publish your hunt for the hungry story. Since 1989, this loosely knit, nationwide organization has seen more than 1 million pounds of game meat have been collected and distributed across the country. The hunter pays the standard processing fee and food banks pick up and distribute the meat within days of its arrival."
http://www.tnugent.com
517-750-9060

National
Law.
American Tort Reform Association (ATRA)
Career Volunteering Description: "Support civil justice reform. Bring greater fairness, predictability and efficiency to the civil justice system through public education and legislative reform. Visit our site to see just what kind of loony lawsuits are out there and how the legal system has grown out of control!"
http://www.atra.org
202 682-1163

National
Law. - If you or someone you know has been touched by cancer, this is for you.
American Cancer Society
Career Volunteering Description: "Become an American Cancer Society grassroots advocate and help shape public policy about cancer related matters and the rights of cancer patients at the local, state, and national levels of government."
www.cancer.org
800.227.2345

National
Law.
Citizens for a Sound Economy(CSE)
Career Volunteering Description: "Get weekly news and the latest info to support free enterprise, lower taxes and limited government."
http://www.cse.org
cse@cse.org
888 JOIN CSE

International

Law.
END WAR, INC.
Career Volunteering Description: "HELP THE LUCOM PLAN LOCATE THE ENEMY. How? Sign and convince others to sign the petition at www.EndWar.com. By the State Department, in accordance with the U.S. Counter Terrorism Law, 22 USC 2708, raising the present ineffective reward to a One-Billion-Dollar Reward for the capture of a terrorist leader or a head of state who is secretly developing weapons of mass destruction or who starts a war. No leader would start a nuclear war, conventional war or terrorist attack if he knew he was going to be hunted down and killed because of the reward."
http://www.endwar.com
peace@endwar.com

National
Law.
Nicole Brown Charitable Foundation
Career Volunteering Description: "Educate yourself about the aspects of domestic violence before practicing law to shield yourself from ignorant senior attorneys. Also Write or call your local, state and federal legislators to promote legislation that would benefit abuse victims who are mostly women and children."
http://www.nbcf.org
info@nbcf.org
(949) 283-5330

National
Law.
NRA ILA
Career Volunteering Description: "Self-defense is a basic human right. Work at the local, state, and federal levels to defend our Second Amendment rights. Champion firearm safety because upholding the Second Amendment carries personal responsibility with the 2.5 million times per year in the U.S. that simply brandishing a firearm was used to prevent a crime such as rape, muggings, domestic violence, robberies, car jackings, and attempted murder. 2 Petition for existing firearms laws be enforced like the 5-year minimum federal prison sentence called Project Exile for those caught with illegal guns."
http://www.nraila.org
800-392-8683

National
Law.
Pink Pistols
Career Volunteering Description: "Armed Gays don't get bashed. Dedicate yourself to the legal, safe, and responsible use of firearms for self-defense of the sexual-minority community. Pink Pistols no longer believes it is the right of those who hate and fear gay, lesbian, bi, trans, or polyandrous persons to use us as targets for their rage. Self-defense is our RIGHT."
www.PinkPistols.org
admin@pinkpistols.org
(617) 686-2564

National
Law.

U.S. Senate
Career Volunteering Description: "Organize petitions and write to Congress on issues that you believe in."
http://www.senate.gov/
202/224-3131

National
Law.
U.S. Constitution Online
Career Volunteering Description: "Re-read The U.S. Constitution online. The U.S. Constitution is truth and justice. Keep U.S. History alive."
http://www.usconstitution.net/

National
Law.
U.S. House of Representatives
Career Volunteering Description: "Organize petitions and write to Congress on issues that you believe in."
http://www.house.gov/
(202) 224-3121

International
Law.
Earth Justice
Career Volunteering Description: "Pro-bono to achieve environmental justice."
http://www.earthjustice.org/
(415) 627-6700

International
Law.
Nuclear Age Peace Foundation
Career Volunteering Description: "Organized petitions and send them to the leaders of the nuclear weapons nations."
http://www.wagingpeace.org
(805) 965-3443

International
Law Enforcement.
Adult Sites Against Child Pornography (ASACP)
Career Volunteering Description: "Report child pornography. Help the adult site industry and the general public make a difference in the ongoing battle against child pornography."
http://www.asacp.org
comments@asacp.org

National
Law Enforcement.
American Muslim Society
Career Volunteering Description: "Report hate crime against Muslim Americans."

http://www.masnet.org/
(703) 998-6525

International
Law Enforcement.
Anti-Child Pornography Organization
Career Volunteering Description: "Report child porn and help stop the sexual exploitation of the world's children."
http://www.antichildporn.org
liaisons@antichildporn.org

National
Law Enforcement.
Citizen Corps - Federal Emergency Management Agency
Career Volunteering Description: "Help individuals prepare themselves and their families for disasters in the Citizen Corps."
http://www.citizencorps.gov
(202) 566-1600

National
Law Enforcement.
DARE (Drug Abuse Resistance Education)
Career Volunteering Description: "Join in on the war on drugs by educating elementary and high school students about drug awareness."
http://www.http://www.dare.org/

International
Law Enforcement.
END WAR, INC.
Career Volunteering Description: "HELP THE LUCOM PLAN LOCATE THE ENEMY. How? Sign and convince others to sign the petition at www.EndWar.com. By the State Department, in accordance with the U.S. Counter Terrorism Law, 22 USC 2708, raising the present ineffective reward to a One-Billion-Dollar Reward for the capture of a terrorist leader or a head of state who is secretly developing weapons of mass destruction or who starts a war. No leader would start a nuclear war, conventional war or terrorist attack if he knew he was going to be hunted down and killed because of the reward."
http://www.endwar.com
peace@endwar.com

National
Law Enforcement.
Marine Corps - Law Enforcement Foundation, Inc.
Career Volunteering Description: "Ultimately fundraise for your children or children of your future comrades. Get involved with raising money for College Scholarships for Children of Heroes... Children of military and law-enforcement officers killed in action."
(877) 606-1775
info@mc-lef.org
http://www.mc-lef.org/

National

Law Enforcement.
National Center for Missing & Exploited Children
Career Volunteering Description: "1. Serve with detectives and officers to find missing children.
2. Help to prevent child sexual exploitation."
http://www.missingkids.com/
703-274-3900

National
Law Enforcement.
National Crime Prevention Council
Career Volunteering Description: "Learn to protect yourself, secure your home and property, safeguard your family and safeguard your school. Help create communities where children can be children and people once isolated by crime and fear can enjoy being a part of a thriving neighborhood."
webmaster@ncpc.org
http://www.ncpc.org
(202) 466-6272

National
Law Enforcement.
National Domestic Violence Hotline
Career Volunteering Description: "Promote 1-800-799-SAFE(7233) to help women get help through crisis intervention, and help battered women through crisis intervention and become a Volunteer Hotline Advocate. "
http://www.ndvh.org
512-453-8117

National
Law Enforcement.
Nicole Brown Charitable Foundation
Career Volunteering Description: "Educate yourself about the aspects of domestic violence before joining the force to shield yourself from ignorant senior officers."
http://www.nbcf.org
info@nbcf.org
(949) 283-5330

National
Law Enforcement.
NRA
Career Volunteering Description: "Teach accident avoidance with the Eddie Eagle gun safety program. If children find a firearm lying out unsupervised, they will learn to: STOP! Don't Touch. Leave the Area. Tell an Adult… Champion firearm safety because upholding the Second Amendment carries personal responsibility with the 2.5 million times per year in the U.S. that simply brandishing a firearm was used to prevent a crime such as rape, muggings, domestic violence, robberies, car jackings, and attempted murder. 2
2. Self-defense is a basic human right. Work at the local, state, and federal levels to defend our Second Amendment rights. Petition for existing firearms laws be enforced

like the 5-year minimum federal prison sentence called Project Exile for those caught with illegal guns."
http://www.nra.org
800-NRA-3888

National
Law Enforcement.
Pink Pistols
Career Volunteering Description: "Armed Gays don't get bashed. Dedicate yourself to the legal, safe, and responsible use of firearms for self-defense of the sexual-minority community. Pink Pistols no longer believes it is the right of those who hate and fear gay, lesbian, bi, trans, or polyandrous persons to use us as targets for their rage. Self-defense is our RIGHT."
www.PinkPistols.org
admin@pinkpistols.org
(617) 686-2564

National
Law Enforcement.
Prevent Child Abuse America
Career Volunteering Description: "Commit to promoting legislation, policies and programs that help to prevent child abuse and neglect, support healthy childhood development, and strengthen families."
http://www.preventchildabuse.org
mailbox@preventchildabuse.org
312-663-3520

National.
Law Enforcement.
ReportChildPorn.com
Career Volunteering Description: "If you come across any Child Porn while enjoying the Internet or receive an illegal email image, make a stance and do your part to stomp out this terrible crime. Submit these webpages to the appropriate law enforcement agencies through the easy to use submission form."
http://www.reportchildporn.com

National
Law Enforcement.
Second Amendment Sisters
"Self-defense is a basic human right. Women: work at the local, state, and federal levels to defend our Second Amendment rights. 'More guns less crime means that States with the largest increases in gun ownership also have the largest drops in violent crimes.' 12"
http://www.sas-aim.org
(877) 271-6216

National
Law Enforcement.
Street Safe Kids

Career Volunteering Description: "Help kids stay safe. Encourage community action. Promote safety awareness. Recognize differences in people. Reduce reasons for violence. Resolve conflict for good of all. Help protect property values in the process."
http://www.compeace.org
compeace@concentric.net
510-530-1319

National
Law Enforcement.
Ted Nugent USA Hunters for the Hungry Program
Career Volunteering Description: "Improve your target practice during your hunt for the hungry. Since 1989, this loosely knit, nationwide organization has seen more than 1 million pounds of game meat have been collected and distributed across the country. The hunter pays the standard processing fee and food banks pick up and distribute the meat within days of its arrival."
http://www.tnugent.com
517-750-9060

National
Law Enforcement.
U.S. Constitution Online
Career Volunteering Description: "Re-read The U.S. Constitution online. The U.S. Constitution is truth and justice. Keep U.S. History alive."
http://www.usconstitution.net/

National
Marine Biology.
Clean Beaches Council
Career Volunteering Description: "Sustain America's beaches."
http://www.cleanbeaches.org
540-373-1436

National
Marine Biology.
National Audubon Society
Career Volunteering Description: "Help identify ways to protect birds, other wildlife and the environment with the new Administration and the new Congress."
http://www.audubon.org
(212) 979 3000

National
Marine Biology.
Ocean Conservancy
Career Volunteering Description: "Help protect our oceans by responding to our Action Alerts."
http://www.oceanconservancy.org
info@oceanconservancy.org
(202) 429-5609

National

Marine Biology.
Wildlife Conservation Society
Career Volunteering Description: "Inspire care for nature, provide leadership in environmental education, and help sustain our planet's biological diversity."
http://wcs.org
718-220-5100

National
Marine Biology.
World Wildlife Fund
Career Volunteering Description: " Save endangered species, preserve wild places, and address global threats."
http://www.worldwildlife.org
1-800-CALL-WWF

International
Marketing.
Aamar Nijer - My Own
Career Volunteering Description: "A solution for poverty in India's Villages is capitalism and entrepreneurship through 'Aamar Nijer Self Dependent Villages.' Develop international import and export marketing and management skills while developing a market in your college or hometown for apparel and traditional crafts from these SPIRITED villagers in India as well as Korak's independent films."
http://www.korakday.com/DirectWork.htm
korak_day@hotmail.com

National
Marketing.
100 Black Men of America, Inc.
Career Volunteering Description: "Serve as a strong force for overcoming the cultural and financial obstacles that have limited the achievements of African-American youth, with a particular emphasis on young African-American males."
http://www.100blackmen.org
(404) 688-5100

National
Marketing.
A Better Chance
Career Volunteering Description: "Help increase the number of well-educated minority youth capable of assuming positions of responsibility and leadership in American society."
http://www.abetterchance.org
(212) 456-1920

National
Marketing.
Alliance To Save Energy
Career Volunteering Description: "Advance the overall goal of moving the United States and the world toward a more energy-efficient, sustainable future."

http://www.ase.org/
202/857-0666

National
Marketing. - If you or someone you know has been touched by cancer, this is for you.
American Cancer Society
Career Volunteering Description: "1. Assist the American Cancer Society in raising money to fund research and support its mission of eliminating cancer and diminishing suffering from cancer. Delivering Daffodils to businesses and schools, forming Relay for Life Teams, attending an Auction or obtaining Auction prizes, are just a few of the Career Volunteer fundraising opportunities available.
2. Help the American Cancer Society local unit in the process of recruiting, training and retaining and recognizing volunteers to do the important work of the Society.
3. Provide clerical and customer service support to a local American Cancer Society unit. Customer service duties include: telephone inquiries, typing, mailings, filing, copying, inventory, materials ordering, stamping of literature, etc.
4. Serve on a committee to plan an American Cancer Society Survivor's Conference.
5. Become an American Cancer Society grassroots advocate or organizer and help shape public policy about cancer related matters and the rights of cancer patients at the local, state, and national levels of government."
www.cancer.org
800.227.2345

National
Marketing.
American Plastics Council
Career Volunteering Description: "Broadcast quality professional format tapes are available to TV stations and can be tailored for use in many communities for plastics recycling."
http://www.americanplasticscouncil.org
800-2-HELP-90

National
Marketing.
Best Buddies
Career Volunteering Description: "Assist individuals to locate and maintain jobs of their own choosing by providing ongoing support and training."
http://www.bestbuddies.org/
(305) 374-2233

National
Marketing.
Citizens Against Government Waste (CAGW)
Career Volunteering Description: "Promote CAGW's mission to eliminate waste, mismanagement, and inefficiency in the federal government."
http://www.cagw.org
membership@cagw.org
202-467-5300

National

Marketing.
Citizens for a Sound Economy (CSE)
Career Volunteering Description: "Get weekly news and the latest info to support free enterprise, lower taxes and limited government."
http://www.cse.org
cse@cse.org
888 JOIN CSE

National
Marketing.
Communities In Schools
Career Volunteering Description: "Offer technology training for the future, career counseling and employment skills, college preparation and scholarship opportunities."
http://www.cisnet.org
cis@cisnet.org
800-CIS-4KIDS

International
Marketing.
END WAR, INC.
Career Volunteering Description: "HELP THE LUCOM PLAN LOCATE THE ENEMY. How? Sign and convince others to sign the petition at www.EndWar.com. By the State Department, in accordance with the U.S. Counter Terrorism Law, 22 USC 2708, raising the present ineffective reward to a One-Billion-Dollar Reward for the capture of a terrorist leader or a head of state who is secretly developing weapons of mass destruction or who starts a war. No leader would start a nuclear war, conventional war or terrorist attack if he knew he was going to be hunted down and killed because of the reward."
http://www.endwar.com
peace@endwar.com

National
Marketing.
Goodwill Industries International, Inc.
Career Volunteering Description: "Volunteer with a business advisory councils that are involved in activities such as developing and reviewing curriculum, providing placement assistance, giving technical advice and networking with other influential members of the business community."
contactus@goodwill.org
http://www.goodwill.org
(240) 333-5200

National
Marketing.
Hugs for Health Foundation
Career Volunteering Description: "Hugs for Health Foundation is building a national database of senior and long-term care facilities seeking volunteers. Help market Hugs for Health Programs to facilities in your area."
http://www.hugs4health.org
JoD@hugs4health.org
562-594-0663

National
Marketing.
National Alliance to End Homelessness
Career Volunteering Description: "Train homeless individuals for employment and help implement the Ten Year Plan to End Homelessness."
naeh@naeh.org
http://www.naeh.org
(202) 638-1526

National
Marketing.
National Coalition for the Homeless
Career Volunteering Description: "Train homeless individuals for employment. Also work and organize an event at a shelter."
info@nationalhomeless.org
http://www.nationalhomeless.org
202.737.6444

National
Marketing.
Nicole Brown Charitable Foundation
Career Volunteering Description: "CALL to PROTECT provides recycled wireless phones pre-programmed to 911 to victims of domestic violence FREE OF CHARGE. These phones serve as an emergency lifeline - one that they might not have access to otherwise. Please help the NBCF's effort to provide all victims of domestic abuse with a wireless phone."
http://www.nbcf.org
info@nbcf.org
(949) 283-5330

National
Marketing.
Renew America
Career Volunteering Description: "Become a part of a network of community and environmental groups, businesses, government leaders and civic activists to exchange ideas and expertise for improving the environment."
http://solstice.crest.org/environment/renew_america
202.721.1545

National
Marketing.
Ronald McDonald House Charities
Career Volunteering Description: "Help manage collecting new toys for visiting children at Ronald McDonald House playrooms."
http://www.rmhc.org
630.623.7048

National

Marketing.
Small Business Administration
Career Volunteering Description: "Help needy families or the elderly organize their finances and taxes."
http://www.sba.gov
800.827.5722

National
Marketing.
Ted Nugent USA Hunters for the Hungry Program
Career Volunteering Description: "Promote a hunt for hungry outing. Since 1989, this loosely knit, nationwide organization has seen more than 1 million pounds of game meat have been collected and distributed across the country. The hunter pays the standard processing fee and food banks pick up and distribute the meat within days of its arrival."
http://www.tnugent.com
517-750-9060

National
Marketing.
Toys for Tots Foundation (Marines)
Career Volunteering Description: "Help collect new, unwrapped toys during October, November and December each year and manage the distribution those toys as Christmas gifts to needy children in the community in which the campaign is conducted."
http://www.toysfortots.org
(703) 640-9433

National
Marketing.
United Way of America
Career Volunteering Description: "Gain business experience and network while fundraising for your local United Way during its campaigns. Search for your local United Way organization on our website."
http://www.UnitedWay.org
(703) 836-7112

National
Marketing.
YouthBuild USA
Career Volunteering Description: "Offer job training, education, counseling, and leadership development opportunities to unemployed and out-of-school young adults, ages 16-24, through the construction and rehabilitation of affordable housing in their own communities."
http://www.youthbuild.org
ybinfo@youthbuild.org
617-623-9900

International
Marketing.
Loving The People

Career Volunteering Description: "We need a creative serious person interested to find new sponsors and volunteers for helping abandoned Romanian children. Please visit our web site."
http://www.pennyjames.btinternet.co.uk/LTP/
004059478501

National
Medical.
AIDS.org
Career Volunteering Description: "Gather information to combat aids and educate students and community members about aids awareness."
http://www.aids.org

National
Medical.
Alzheimer's Association
Career Volunteering Description: "1. Help improve the lives of families affected by dementia through research, education, and patient care.
2. Provide education and support for people diagnosed with the condition, their families, and caregivers."
http://www.alz.org
info@alz.org
800.272.3900

National
Medical. - If you or someone you know has been touched by cancer, this is for you.
American Cancer Society
Career Volunteering Description: "1. Become an American Cancer Society Road to Recovery volunteer driver taking patients to chemotherapy or radiation treatments and develop a better bedside manner before actually practicing medicine. Training involved.
2. Distribute American Cancer Society Reach to Recovery and information to doctor's offices, pharmacies, and dentists. Set meetings to play the powerful Reach to Recovery video.
3. Serve on a committee to plan an American Cancer Society Survivor's Conference.
4. Distribute brochures at urologist offices, golf courses, bowling alleys, etc. to promote the American Cancer Society Man to Man meetings that provide education and the opportunity to network with others who have prostate cancer, where support is also available.
5. Bring the message of the importance of annual mammograms to groups of women through the American Cancer Society Tell A Friend program. Training involved.
6. Speak about American Cancer Society Early Detection guidelines through the American Cancer Society Ambassador Program to community groups, community health fairs, volunteer fairs, civic organization meetings, coalition meetings, screenings, etc. Training involved.
7. Speak about American Cancer Society Patient Services through the American Cancer Society Ambassador Program to community groups, community health fairs, volunteer fairs, civic organization meetings, coalition meetings, screenings, etc. Training involved.
8. Assist with Cancer Control activities at American Cancer Society Relay for Life. Involves training.

9. Individuals can help the American Cancer Society advocate for Comprehensive School Health Education to develop school health advisory councils in their local school districts. Involves training."
www.cancer.org
800.227.2345

National
Medical.
American Diabetes Association
Career Volunteering Description: "Provide information and other services to people with diabetes, their families, health care professionals and the public. Start by supporting diabetes research, information or advocacy."
http://www.diabetes.org
AskADA@diabetes.org
800-DIABETES

National
Medical.
American Heart Association
Career Volunteering Description: "Learn CPR and maybe teach CPR."
http://www.americanheart.org/
800-AHA-USA1

National and International
Medical.
American Red Cross
Career Volunteering Description: "Helping people in emergencies, providing half the nation's blood supply, teaching first aid and CPR courses, delivering emergency messages to members of the military, organizing programs for the elderly, for the youth…"
http://www.redcross.org
703-206-6011

National and International
Medical.
amfAR (American Foundation for AIDS Research)
Career Volunteering Description: "Help prevent HIV infection and the disease and death associated with it, and protect the human rights of all people threatened by the epidemic of HIV/AIDS."
http://www.amfar.org
teri.lujan@amfar.org
800-39-amfAR

National
Medical.
Arthritis Foundation
Career Volunteering Description: "Support the more than 100 types of arthritis and related conditions with advocacy, programs, services and research. Teach classes, leading support groups, organize events and more."
http://www.arthritis.org

800-283-7800

National
Medical.
CAPS(Center for AIDS Prevention Studies)
Career Volunteering Description: "Reduce adolescents' risk for HIV infection by using peer role models to advocate for responsible decision-making, healthy values and norms, and improved communication skills."
http://www.caps.ucsf.edu

National
Medical.
Project Prevention
Children Requiring a Caring Community
Career Volunteering Description: "Reduce the number of drug and alcohol related pregnancies to zero. Unlike incarceration, Project Prevention is extremely cost effective and does not punish the participants."
(714) 901-9862
info@projectprevention.org
http://www.projectprevention.org

National
Meteorology.
Environmental Defense Fund
Career Volunteering Description: "Reduce pollution through activism."
http://www.environmentaldefense.org
800-684-3322

National
Meteorology.
Federal Emergency Management Agency
Career Volunteering Description: "Help individuals prepare themselves and their families for tornados, hurricanes, severe thunderstorms, flash floods, blizzards and other natural disasters."
http://www.fema.gov
(202) 566-1600

National
Music. - If you or someone you know has been touched by cancer, this is for you.
American Cancer Society
Career Volunteering Description: "If you or your band is good, put on benefit gigs to raise money at the American Cancer Society Relay for Life. You will gain publicity not only performing, but also helping a good cause."
www.cancer.org
800.227.2345

National
Music.
Communities In Schools

Career Volunteering Description: "Work with a child as a tutor or mentor, and help with after-school and extended-hours programs."
http://www.cisnet.org
cis@cisnet.org
800-CIS-4KIDS

National.
Music.
Flock of Angels & Nicole Brown Charitable Foundation
Career Volunteering Description: "'Virtual Angels' volunteer from the comfort of their home or office. After being introduced, Angels are assigned to smaller 'Flocks' that are responsible for individual projects such as: Anti Violence Music and Art's Festival, Memorial Season, Nicole's Memorial, Live Events and more."
http://www.flockofangels.org
info@flockofangels.org
949-588-6262

National
Nursing.
AIDS.org
Career Volunteering Description: "Gather information to combat aids and educate students and community members about aids awareness."
http://www.aids.org

National
Nursing.
Alzheimer's Association
Career Volunteering Description: "1. Help improve the lives of families affected by dementia through research, education, and patient care.
2. Provide education and support for people diagnosed with the condition, their families, and caregivers."
http://www.alz.org
info@alz.org
800.272.3900

National
Nursing.
American Diabetes Association
Career Volunteering Description: "Provide information and other services to people with diabetes, their families, health care professionals and the public. Start by supporting diabetes research, information or advocacy."
http://www.diabetes.org
AskADA@diabetes.org
800-DIABETES

National
Nursing.
American Social Health Association
Career Volunteering Description: "Help stop all sexually transmitted diseases."
http://www.ashastd.org

919.361.8400

National
Nursing. - If you or someone you know has been touched by cancer, this is for you.
American Cancer Society
Career Volunteering Description: "1. Serve on a committee to plan an American Cancer Society Survivor's Conference.
2. Distribute American Cancer Society Reach to Recovery and information to doctor's offices, pharmacies, and dentists. Set meetings to play the powerful Reach to Recovery video.
3. Distribute brochures at urologist offices, golf courses, bowling alleys, etc. to promote the American Cancer Society Man to Man meetings that provide education and the opportunity to network with others who have prostate cancer, where support is also available.
4. Speak about American Cancer Society Early Detection guidelines through the American Cancer Society Ambassador Program to community groups, community health fairs, volunteer fairs, civic organization meetings, coalition meetings, screenings, etc. Training involved.
5. Speak about American Cancer Society Patient Services through the American Cancer Society Ambassador Program to community groups, community health fairs, volunteer fairs, civic organization meetings, coalition meetings, screenings, etc. Training involved.
6. Assist with Cancer Control activities at American Cancer Society Relay for Life. Involves training.
7. Bring the message of the importance of annual mammograms to groups of women through the American Cancer Society Tell A Friend program. Training involved.
www.cancer.org
800.227.2345

National
Nursing.
American Heart Assn
Career Volunteering Description: "Learn CPR and maybe teach CPR."
http://www.americanheart.org/
800-AHA-USA1

National and International
Nursing.
amfAR (American Foundation for AIDS Research)
Career Volunteering Description: "Help prevent HIV infection and the disease and death associated with it, and protect the human rights of all people threatened by the epidemic of HIV/AIDS."
http://www.amfar.org
teri.lujan@amfar.org
800-39-amfAR

National
Nursing.
Arthritis Foundation

Career Volunteering Description: "Support the more than 100 types of arthritis and related conditions with advocacy, programs, services and research. Teach classes, leading support groups, organize events and more."
http://www.arthritis.org
800-283-7800

National
Nursing.
Family Violence Prevention Fund
Career Volunteering Description: "Educate the nation about the needs of children and encourage preventive investment before children get sick or into trouble, drop out of school, or suffer family breakdown."
http://www.endabuse.org
(415) 252-8900

National
Nursing.
Project Prevention
Children Requiring a Caring Community
Career Volunteering Description: "Reduce the number of drug and alcohol related pregnancies to zero. Unlike incarceration, Project Prevention is extremely cost effective and does not punish the participants."
(714) 901-9862
info@projectprevention.org
http://www.projectprevention.org

National
Oceanography.
American Cetacean Society
Career Volunteering Description: "Work to protect whales, dolphins, porpoises, and their habitats through education, conservation and research."
http://www.acsonline.org
310-548-6279

National
Oceanography.
National Audubon Society
Career Volunteering Description: "Help identify ways to protect coastal birds, other coastal wildlife and the environment with the new Administration and the new Congress."
http://www.audubon.org
(212) 979 3000

National
Oceanography.
Ocean Conservancy
Career Volunteering Description: "Help protect our oceans by responding to our Action Alerts."
!http://www.oceanconservancy.org
info@oceanconservancy.org

(202) 429-5609

National
Oceanography.
World Wildlife Fund
Career Volunteering Description: "Save endangered species, preserve wild places, and address global threats."
http://www.worldwildlife.org
1-800-CALL-WWF

National
Pharmacy.
Alzheimer's Association
Career Volunteering Description: "1. Help improve the lives of families affected by dementia through research, education, and patient care.
2. Provide education and support for people diagnosed with the condition, their families, and caregivers."
http://www.alz.org
info@alz.org
800.272.3900

National
Pharmacy. - If you or someone you know has been touched by cancer, this is for you.
American Cancer Society
Career Volunteering Description: "1. Speak about American Cancer Society Patient Services through the American Cancer Society Ambassador Program to community groups, community health fairs, volunteer fairs, civic organization meetings, coalition meetings, screenings, etc. Training involved.
2. Speak about American Cancer Society Early Detection guidelines through the American Cancer Society Ambassador Program to community groups, community health fairs, volunteer fairs, civic organization meetings, coalition meetings, screenings, etc. Training involved.
3. Assist with Cancer Control activities at American Cancer Society Relay for Life. Involves training.
4. Speak at an American Cancer Society Youth Tobacco Leadership event and a local school health advisory council about the negative chemical reactions that take place in the body after smoking a cigarette or chewing spit tobacco. Involves training."
www.cancer.org
800.227.2345

National
Pharmacy.
American Diabetes Association
Career Volunteering Description: "Provide information and other services to people with diabetes, their families, health care professionals and the public. Start by supporting diabetes research, information or advocacy."
http://www.diabetes.org
AskADA@diabetes.org
800-DIABETES

National and International
Pharmacy.
amfAR (American Foundation for AIDS Research)
Career Volunteering Description: "Help prevent HIV infection and the disease and death associated with it, and protect the human rights of all people threatened by the epidemic of HIV/AIDS."
http://www.amfar.org
teri.lujan@amfar.org
800-39-amfAR

National
Pharmacy.
American Social Health Assn
Career Volunteering Description: "Help stop all sexually transmitted diseases."
http://www.ashastd.org
919.361.8400

National
Pharmacy.
Arthritis Foundation
Career Volunteering Description: "Support the more than 100 types of arthritis and related conditions with advocacy, programs, services and research. Teach classes, leading support groups, organize events and more."
http://www.arthritis.org
800-283-7800

National
Pharmacy.
CAPS (Ctr for AIDS Prevention Studies)
Career Volunteering Description: "Reduce adolescents' risk for HIV infection by using peer role models to advocate for responsible decision-making, healthy values and norms, and improved communication skills."
http://www.caps.ucsf.edu

National
Physical Education. - If you or someone you know has been touched by cancer, this is for you.
American Cancer Society
Career Volunteering Description: "1. Speak about American Cancer Society Patient Services physical activity guidelines through the American Cancer Society Ambassador Program to community groups, community health fairs, volunteer fairs, civic organization meetings, coalition meetings, screenings, etc. Training involved.
2. Speak about American Cancer Society Preventative, physical activity guidelines through the American Cancer Society Ambassador Program to community groups, community health fairs, volunteer fairs, civic organization meetings, coalition meetings, screenings, etc. Training involved.
3. Individuals can help the American Cancer Society advocate for Comprehensive School Health Education to develop school health advisory councils in their local school districts. Involves training.
4. Become a Team Captain at the American Cancer Society's signature event, Relay for Life, to not only help organize the 24 hour walking or running event, but to raise funds to

fight cancer. What a better major to remind participants to drink plenty of fluids or take a break and get out of the sun."
www.cancer.org
800.227.2345

National
Physical Education.
American Heart Association
Career Volunteering Description: "Learn CPR and maybe teach CPR."
http://www.americanheart.org/
800-AHA-USA1

National
Physical Education.
Arthritis Foundation
Career Volunteering Description: "Support the more than 100 types of arthritis and related conditions with advocacy, programs, services and research. Teach classes, leading support groups, organize events and more."
http://www.arthritis.org
800-283-7800

National
Physical Education.
Communities In Schools
Career Volunteering Description: "Work with a child as a tutor or mentor, and help with after-school and extended-hours programs."
http://www.cisnet.org
cis@cisnet.org
800-CIS-4KIDS

National
Physical Education.
Special Olympics
Career Volunteering Description: "Help organize events at your local Special Olympics."
http://www.specialolympics.org/
202.628.3630

National
Physical Education.
YWCA
Career Volunteering Description: "Volunteers engage in all types of activities, including mentoring."
http://www.ywca.org
(212) 273-7800

International
Physics.
Nuclear Age Peace Fdn

Career Volunteering Description: "Organized petitions and send them to the leaders of the nuclear weapons nations."
http://www.wagingpeace.org
(805) 965-3443

National
Political Science. - If you or someone you know has been touched by cancer, this is for you.
American Cancer Society
Career Volunteering Description: "Become an American Cancer Society grassroots advocate and help shape public policy about cancer related matters and the rights of cancer patients at the local, state, and national levels of government."
www.cancer.org
800.227.2345

National
Political Science.
American Tort Reform Association (ATRA)
Career Volunteering Description: "Support civil justice reform. Bring greater fairness, predictability and efficiency to the civil justice system through public education and legislative reform. Visit our site to see just what kind of loony lawsuits are out there and how the legal system has grown out of control!"
http://www.atra.org
202 682-1163

National
Political Science.
Citizen Corps - Federal Emergency Management Agency
Career Volunteering Description: "Help individuals prepare themselves and their families for disasters in the Citizen Corps."
http://www.citizencorps.gov
(202) 566-1600

National
Political Science.
Citizens Against Government Waste (CAGW)
Career Volunteering Description: "Stay updated with the latest on how Washington is wasting your money, and action alerts so that you can take part in urgent tax and spending battles."
http://www.cagw.org
membership@cagw.org
202-467-5300

National
Political Science.
Citizens for a Sound Economy(CSE)
Career Volunteering Description: Get weekly news and the latest info to support free enterprise, lower taxes and limited government."
http://www.cse.org
cse@cse.org
888 JOIN CSE

National
Political Science.
Election.com
Career Volunteering Description: "Motivate people to register and vote."
http://www.election.com

International
Political Science.
END WAR, INC.
Career Volunteering Description: "HELP THE LUCOM PLAN LOCATE THE ENEMY. How? Sign and convince others to sign the petition at www.EndWar.com. By the State Department, in accordance with the U.S. Counter Terrorism Law, 22 USC 2708, raising the present ineffective reward to a One-Billion-Dollar Reward for the capture of a terrorist leader or a head of state who is secretly developing weapons of mass destruction or who starts a war. No leader would start a nuclear war, conventional war or terrorist attack if he knew he was going to be hunted down and killed because of the reward."
http://www.endwar.com
peace@endwar.com

National
Political Science.
Nicole Brown Charitable Foundation
Career Volunteering Description: "Write or call your local, state and federal legislators to promote legislation that would benefit abuse victims who are mostly women and children."
http://www.nbcf.org
info@nbcf.org
(949) 283-5330

National
Political Science.
NRA ILA
Career Volunteering Description: "Self-defense is a basic human right. Work at the local, state, and federal levels to defend our Second Amendment rights. Champion firearm safety because upholding the Second Amendment carries personal responsibility with the 2.5 million times per year in the U.S. that simply brandishing a firearm was used to prevent a crime such as rape, muggings, domestic violence, robberies, car jackings, and attempted murder. 2 Petition for existing firearms laws be enforced like the 5-year minimum federal prison sentence called Project Exile for those caught with illegal guns."
http://www.nraila.org
800-392-8683

National
Political Science.
Pink Pistols
Career Volunteering Description: "Armed Gays don't get bashed. Dedicate yourself to the legal, safe, and responsible use of firearms for self-defense of the sexual-minority community. Pink Pistols no longer believes it is the right of those who hate and fear gay,

lesbian, bi, trans, or polyandrous persons to use us as targets for their rage. Self-defense is our RIGHT."
www.PinkPistols.org
admin@pinkpistols.org
(617) 686-2564

National
Political Science.
Renew America
Career Volunteering Description: "Become a part of a network of community and environmental groups, businesses, government leaders and civic activists to exchange ideas and expertise for improving the environment."
http://solstice.crest.org/environment/renew_america
202.721.1545

National
Political Science.
Second Amendment Sisters
"Self-defense is a basic human right. Women: work at the local, state, and federal levels to defend our Second Amendment rights. 'More guns less crime means that States with the largest increases in gun ownership also have the largest drops in violent crimes.' 12"
http://www.sas-aim.org
(877) 271-6216

National
Political Science.
U.S. Constitution Online
Career Volunteering Description: "Re-read The U.S. Constitution online. The U.S. Constitution is truth and justice. Keep U.S. History alive."
http://www.usconstitution.net/

National
Political Science.
U.S. Senate
Career Volunteering Description: "Organize petitions and write to Congress on issues that you believe in."
http://www.senate.gov/
202/224-3131

International
Political Science.
Nuclear Age Peace Foundation
Career Volunteering Description: "Organized petitions and send them to the leaders of the nuclear weapons nations."
http://www.wagingpeace.org
(805) 965-3443

National
Psychology.

Alzheimer's Association
Career Volunteering Description: "1. Help improve the lives of families affected by dementia through research, education, and patient care.
2. Provide education and support for people diagnosed with the condition, their families, and caregivers."
http://www.alz.org
info@alz.org
800.272.3900

National
Psychology. - If you or someone you know has been touched by cancer, this is for you.
American Cancer Society
Career Volunteering Description: "1. Help recruit American Cancer Society Cancer Survivor Network Volunteers who play a vital role in pre-recording their powerful testimonials of surviving cancer that offers hope to others with cancer.
2. Distribute American Cancer Society Look Good, Feel Better brochures to hair salons, wig salons or prosthesis stores in your area. Set meetings to play the powerful video that describes the CAMARADERIE and rise in self-esteem that women experience while learning beauty techniques to combat the appearance related side effects of cancer treatment."
www.cancer.org
800.227.2345

National
Psychology.
American Muslim Council
Career Volunteering Description: "Educate to not retaliate against Muslim Americans. Muslim Americans condemn terrorist attacks as un-Islamic, barbaric, and inhumane."
http://www.amconline.org
202 789 2262

National
Psychology.
Childhelp USA
Career Volunteering Description: "Provide counseling referrals for abused children."
http://www.childhelpusa.org/
1-800-4-A-CHILD

National
Psychology.
Children's Defense Fund
Career Volunteering Description: "Offer basic parenting skill classes to teach teenage parents how to properly raise a child."
http://www.childrensdefense.org
202.628.8787

International
Psychology.
Conflict Resolution Center International
Career Volunteering Description: "Promote non-violent conflict resolution."

http://www.conflictres.org/
412 687 6232

National
Psychology.
Family Violence Prevention Fund
Career Volunteering Description: "Educate the nation about the needs of children and encourage preventive investment before children get sick or into trouble, drop out of school, or suffer family breakdown."
http://www.endabuse.org
(415) 252-8900

National
Psychology.
Lutheran Services In America
Career Volunteering Description: "Offer a wide spectrum of human services to children and families, to older people and to people with disabilities."
http://www.lutheranservices.org
800-664-3848

National
Psychology.
National Campaign To Prevent Teen Pregnancy
Career Volunteer Description: "Educate teens 13 and up to improve the well-being of children, youth, and families by reducing teen pregnancy."
http://www.teenpregnancy.org
(202) 478-8500
campaign@teenpregnancy.org

National
Psychology.
National Council on Alcoholism and Drug Dependence, Inc. (NCADD)
Career Volunteering Description: "Provide education, information, help and hope to the public. Advocate prevention, intervention and treatment through offices in New York and Washington, and a nationwide network of Affiliates."
http://www.ncadd.org
212.269.7797

National
Psychology.
National Domestic Violence Hotline
Career Volunteering Description: "Promote 1-800-799-SAFE(7233) to help women get help through crisis intervention, and help battered women through crisis intervention and become a Volunteer Hotline Advocate."
512-453-8117
http://www.ndvh.org

National
Psychology.

National Mental Health Association
Career Volunteering Description: "Work to improve the mental health of all Americans, especially the 54 million individuals with mental disorders, through advocacy, education, research and service."
http://www.nmha.org
703/684-7722

National.
Psychology.
Nicole Brown Charitable Foundation
Career Volunteering Description: "Educate yourself about the aspects of domestic violence and shield yourself from ignorant colleagues and administrators when entering the workforce. You can also volunteer their public speaking skills at colleges, high schools, community centers, for corporations, and virtually anywhere in the community."
http://www.nbcf.org
info@nbcf.org
(949) 283-5330

National
Psychology.
Prevent Child Abuse America
Career Volunteering Description: "Commit to promoting legislation, policies and programs that help to prevent child abuse and neglect, support healthy childhood development, and strengthen families."
http://www.preventchildabuse.org
mailbox@preventchildabuse.org
312-663-3520

National
Psychology.
Project Prevention
Children Requiring a Caring Community
Career Volunteering Description: "Reduce the number of drug and alcohol related pregnancies to zero. Unlike incarceration, Project Prevention is extremely cost effective and does not punish the participants."
(714) 901-9862
info@projectprevention.org
http://www.projectprevention.org

National
Psychology.
YouthBuild USA
Career Volunteering Description: "Offer counseling and leadership development opportunities to unemployed and out-of-school young adults, ages 16-24, through the construction and rehabilitation of affordable housing in their own communities."
http://www.youthbuild.org
ybinfo@youthbuild.org
617-623-9900

National

Respiratory Therapy.
American Lung Association
Career Volunteering Description: "Fight lung disease by teaching children how to avoid asthma attacks, educating youngsters about the dangers of tobacco and raising money for lung disease research."
http://www.lungusa.org
212-315-8700

National
Respiratory Therapy. - If you or someone you know has been touched by cancer, this is for you.
American Cancer Society
Career Volunteering Description: "1. Speak at an American Cancer Society Youth Tobacco Leadership event and a local school health advisory council about the negative chemical reactions that take place in the lungs and body after smoking a cigarette. Involves training.
2. Individuals can help the American Cancer Society advocate for Comprehensive School Health Education to develop school health advisory councils in their local school districts. Involves training."
www.cancer.org
800.227.2345

National
Safety Sciences.
American Assoc of Homes & Services for the Aging
Career Volunteering Description: "Develop a home safety for seniors check list. Prevent injuries by inspecting and fixing problems in homes owned by the elderly."
(202) 783-2242
member@aahsa.org
http://www.aahsa.org

National
Safety Sciences.
CARE (Cooperative for Assistance and Relief Everywhere)
Career Volunteering Description: "Work with poor communities to find lasting solutions to poverty and infrastructure. Help the world's poor with enough clean water to drink."
info@care.org
http://www.care.org
404-681-2552

National
Safety Sciences.
Federal Emergency Management Agency
Career Volunteering Description: "Help individuals prepare themselves and their families for disasters."
http://www.fema.gov
(202) 566-1600

National
Safety Sciences.

NFPA (National Fire Protection Association)
Career Volunteering Description: "Educate your community about fire and life safety through its Risk Watch®, Learn Not to Burn®, and Fire Prevention Week Programs."
http://www.nfpa.org
education@nfpa.org
617 770-3000

National
Sociology.
A Better Chance
Career Volunteering Description: "Help increase the number of well-educated minority youth capable of assuming positions of responsibility and leadership in American society."
http://www.abetterchance.org
(212) 456-1920

National
Sociology.
Alzheimer's Association
Career Volunteering Description: "1. Help improve the lives of families affected by dementia through research, education, and patient care.
2. Provide education and support for people diagnosed with the condition, their families, and caregivers."
http://www.alz.org
info@alz.org
800.272.3900

International
Sociology.
Anti-Child Pornography Organization
Career Volunteering Description: "Report child porn and help stop the sexual exploitation of the world's children."
http://www.antichildporn.org
liaisons@antichildporn.org

National
Sociology.
The ARC
Career Volunteering Description: "Provide programs and services to children and adults with mental retardation and related developmental disabilities and their families."
Info@thearc.org
http://www.thearc.org
301-565-3842

National
Sociology. - If you or someone you know has been touched by cancer, this is for you.
American Cancer Society
Career Volunteering Description: "1. Help recruit American Cancer Society Cancer Survivor Network Volunteers who play a vital role in pre-recording their powerful testimonials of surviving cancer that offers hope to others with cancer.

2. Distribute American Cancer Society Look Good, Feel Better brochures to hair salons, wig salons or prosthesis stores in your area. Set meetings to play the powerful video that describes the CAMARADERIE and rise in self-esteem that women experience while learning beauty techniques to combat the appearance related side effects of cancer treatment.
www.cancer.org
800.227.2345

National
Sociology.
American Diabetes Association
Career Volunteering Description: "Provide information and other services to people with diabetes, their families, health care professionals and the public. Start by supporting diabetes research, information or advocacy."
http://www.diabetes.org
AskADA@diabetes.org
800-DIABETES

National and International
Sociology.
amfAR (American Foundation for AIDS Research)
Career Volunteering Description: "Help prevent HIV infection and the disease and death associated with it, and protect the human rights of all people threatened by the epidemic of HIV/AIDS."
http://www.amfar.org
teri.lujan@amfar.org
800-39-amfAR

National
Sociology.
Arthritis Foundation
Career Volunteering Description: "Support the more than 100 types of arthritis and related conditions with advocacy, programs, services and research. Teach classes, leading support groups, organize events and more."
http://www.arthritis.org
800-283-7800

National
Sociology.
Best Buddies
Career Volunteering Description: "Enhance the lives of people with mental retardation by providing opportunities for one-to-one friendships and integrated employment."
http://www.bestbuddies.org/
(305) 374-2233

National and International
Sociology.
CARE (Cooperative for Assistance and Relief Everywhere)
Career Volunteering Description: "Work with poor communities to find lasting solutions to poverty. Help the world's poor with enough food to eat and clean water to drink,

having access to health care, basic education and economic opportunity, and having the ability to participate in decisions affecting one's family and community."
info@care.org
http://www.care.org
404-681-2552

National
Sociology.
Catholic Charities USA
Career Volunteering Description: "Reduce poverty, support families and empower communities."
http://www.catholiccharitiesinfo.org
(703) 549-1390

National
Sociology.
Family Violence Prevention Fund
Career Volunteering Description: "Educate the nation about the needs of children and encourage preventive investment before children get sick or into trouble, drop out of school, or suffer family breakdown."
http://www.endabuse.org
(415) 252-8900

National.
Sociology.
Flock of Angels & Nicole Brown Charitable Foundation
Career Volunteering Description: "'Virtual Angels' volunteer from the comfort of their home or office. After being introduced, Angels are assigned to smaller 'Flocks' that are responsible for individual projects such as: Web Research, Proof Reading, Anti Violence Music and Art's Festival, Memorial Season, Nicole's Memorial, Anti Violence Newsletter, Live Events and more."
http://www.flockofangels.org
info@flockofangels.org
949-588-6262

National
Sociology.
Lutheran Services In America
Career Volunteering Description: "Offer a wide spectrum of human services to children and families, to older people and to people with disabilities."
http://www.lutheranservices.org
800-664-3848

National
Sociology.
National Alliance to End Homelessness
Career Volunteering Description: "Train homeless individuals for employment and help implement the Ten Year Plan to End Homelessness."
naeh@naeh.org
http://www.naeh.org

(202) 638-1526

National
Sociology.
National Campaign To Prevent Teen Pregnancy
Career Volunteer Description: "Educate teens 13 and up to improve the well-being of children, youth, and families by reducing teen pregnancy."
http://www.teenpregnancy.org
(202) 478-8500
campaign@teenpregnancy.org

National
Sociology.
National Coalition for the Homeless
Career Volunteering Description: "1. Train homeless individuals for employment.
2. Work and organize an event at a shelter.
3. Find out if there are children who could benefit from tutors or mentors."
info@nationalhomeless.org
http://www.nationalhomeless.org
202.737.6444

National
Sociology.
National Domestic Violence Hotline
Career Volunteering Description: "Promote 1-800-799-SAFE(7233) to help women get help through crisis intervention, and help battered women through crisis intervention and become a Volunteer Hotline Advocate."
512-453-8117
http://www.ndvh.org

National.
Sociology.
Nicole Brown Charitable Foundation
Career Volunteering Description: "Educate yourself about the aspects of domestic violence and shield yourself from ignorant colleagues and administrators when entering the workforce. You can also volunteer their public speaking skills at colleges, high schools, community centers, for corporations, and virtually anywhere in the community."
http://www.nbcf.org
info@nbcf.org
(949) 283-5330

National
Sociology.
Prevent Child Abuse America
Career Volunteering Description: "Commit to promoting legislation, policies and programs that help to prevent child abuse and neglect, support healthy childhood development, and strengthen families."
http://www.preventchildabuse.org
mailbox@preventchildabuse.org

312-663-3520

National
Sociology.
Project Prevention
Children Requiring a Caring Community
Career Volunteering Description: "Reduce the number of drug and alcohol related pregnancies to zero. Unlike incarceration, Project Prevention is extremely cost effective and does not punish the participants."
(714) 901-9862
info@projectprevention.org
http://www.projectprevention.org

National
Sociology.
YouthBuild USA
Career Volunteering Description: "Offer job training, education, counseling, and leadership development opportunities to unemployed and out-of-school young adults, ages 16-24, through the construction and rehabilitation of affordable housing in their own communities."
http://www.youthbuild.org
ybinfo@youthbuild.org
617-623-9900

International
Sociology.
Amesty Intl'
Career Volunteering Description: "Protect and promote human rights."
http://www.aiusa.org
212 807 8400

International
Sociology.
Loving The People
Career Volunteering Description: "Help develop our social work program in order to make it more and more efficient for the help of the abandoned children."
http://www.pennyjames.btinternet.co.uk/LTP/
004059478501

National
Special Education.
The ARC
Career Volunteering Description: "Provide programs and services to children and adults with mental retardation and related developmental disabilities and their families."
Info@thearc.org
http://www.thearc.org
301-565-3842

National

Special Education.
Best Buddies
Career Volunteering Description: "Enhance the lives of people with mental retardation by providing opportunities for one-to-one friendships and integrated employment."
http://www.bestbuddies.org/
(305) 374-2233

National
Special Education.
Easter Seals
Career Volunteering Description: "Make a difference and help people with disabilities achieve their goals. Volunteer your time to share your talents, whether performing office work, volunteering at events and camps, or another way you can help."
www.easter-seals.org
800-221-6827

National
Special Education.
National Multiple Sclerosis Society
Career Volunteering Description: "Aid to improve speech patterns, enunciation, and oral communication in general with those with M.S."
http://www.nmss.org

National
Special Education.
Special Olympics
Career Volunteering Description: "Help organize events for more than one million children and adults with mental retardation."
http://www.specialolympics.org/
202.628.3630

National
Special Education.
United Cerebral Palsy
Career Volunteering Description: "Advance the independence, productivity and full citizenship of people with cerebral palsy and other disabilities."
http://www.ucp.org
(800) USA-5-UCP

National
Sports Medicine. - If you or someone you know has been touched by cancer, this is for you.
American Cancer Society
Career Volunteering Description: " 1. Speak about American Cancer Society Patient Services physical activity guidelines through the American Cancer Society Ambassador Program to community groups, community health fairs, volunteer fairs, civic organization meetings, coalition meetings, screenings, etc. Training involved.
2. Speak about American Cancer Society Preventative, physical activity guidelines through the American Cancer Society Ambassador Program to community groups,

community health fairs, volunteer fairs, civic organization meetings, coalition meetings, screenings, etc. Training involved.
3. Become a Team Captain at the American Cancer Society's signature event, Relay for Life, to not only help organize the 24 hour walking or running event, but to raise funds to fight cancer. What a better major to remind participants to drink plenty of fluids or take a break and get out of the sun."
www.cancer.org
800.227.2345

National
Sports Medicine.
Arthritis Foundation
Career Volunteering Description: "Support the more than 100 types of arthritis and related conditions with advocacy, programs, services and research. Teach classes, leading support groups, organize events and more."
http://www.arthritis.org
800-283-7800

National
Sports Medicine.
Special Olympics
Career Volunteering Description: "Help organize events at your local Special Olympics."
http://www.specialolympics.org/
202.628.3630

National.
Veterinary. Zoology.
American Humane Association
Career Volunteering Description: "Prevent cruelty, abuse, neglect, and exploitation of children and animals, and assures that their interests and well-being are fully, effectively, and humanely guaranteed by an aware and caring society."
http://www.americanhumane.org
animal@americanhumane.org
(303) 925-9476

National
Zoology.
National Audubon Society
Career Volunteering Description: "Help identify ways to protect birds, other wildlife and the environment with the new Administration and the new Congress."
http://www.audubon.org
(212) 979 3000

National
Zoology.
World Wildlife Fund
Career Volunteering Description: "Save endangered species, and preserve wild places."
http://www.worldwildlife.org
1-800-CALL-WWF

Chapter Eleven: A Lesson On A Few Interviewing Tips

Remember to dress for success... **The interviewer will** probably ask you these questions in order that are listed below. It is perfect if the interviewer right off the bat says, "So tell me about yourself" because you can set the rest of the agenda for the interview. If they ask the "tell me about yourself" question, start your response by answering the questions in order that are listed below without waiting for the interviewer to ask them.

However, One of the most important things you can do is LISTEN. Try to ask the interviewer what THEY are looking for, sit back and LISTEN. It's human nature that people like to talk about themselves, so walk away from the interview making an impression as a great listener.

Q: Why are you looking? (Summarize your position. If you were laid off, do not blame.) Here is what happened to me as an example in my answer:

A: "The area that I was recruited for was a new concept and division within Choice One Communications, and in spite of the fact that we were making some in roads, our division did not have full corporate support and was downsized."

Q: What am I looking for? (Highlight your skills first, like your Career Volunteering experience, and briefly explain what your primary goal is for your career, and industry area of interest.) Again, another example in my answer:

A: "I'm looking for an opportunity where I can use my skills in project management, internal and external Internet marketing, people management skills and creative writing and communications skills to make an impact in people's lives. The areas that would be of interest to me are a university setting, government, non-profit or foundation and the private sector." I would then start talking about some of my specific accomplishments & experiences at Choice One Communications, including telecommuting twice a week, since that was an important perk. I would also talk about my public speaking experience with Career Volunteering.

Q: What type of salary are you looking for? (State your salary range, but never bring money up. Let the interviewer do that.)

A: "Well, I know what the market is like. I would expect that you would make a fair offer."

I would highly recommend that you learn about street-smart strategies for landing your dream job and creating a successful future by purchasing the book, FROM COLLEGE TO THE REAL WORLD, by James Malinchak. It is a must read for every college student! James shares unique strategies that teach students how to creatively package, market and sell themselves to employers. This book teaches students how to instantly separate themselves from the crowd so they can beat out any candidate for any position. The strategies in this book have one objective: TO GET STUDENTS HIRED!

Closing Remark

My friend Tyler Durden once said, "We are the middle children of history, raised by television to believe that someday we'll be millionaires and movie stars and rock stars, but be won't. And we're just learning this fact." Remember you can always turn off the T.V., move forward, evolve and do the work.

If you choose to join our cause, I'll be personally very grateful.

Thanks for your time,
Mark Stefanick

Career Volunteering Action Check List

[ ]   DECIDE WHAT YOU WANT TO DO.
• Ask yourself, what is your major and what type of volunteer work would you like to do pertaining to your major or curriculum?
• Decide what you want to do, and for how many hours a week.
• Make your own flexible schedule.

[ ]   LOCATE WHERE YOU WANT TO VOLUNTEER.
• Look in your local phone book for the Guide To Human Services listing. This is a great resource that lists not-for-profit agencies in alphabetical order where you can Career Volunteer. The categories usually are: Abuse and Assault; Adoption; Alcohol and Drug Problems; Camps; Children and Youth; Community Services; Consumer Problems; Day Care; The Disabled; Discrimination; Education and Enrichment; Family and Marriage; Food; Health; Home Health Care; Hospice; Hospitals; Hotlines; Housing; Job Problems; Language and Communication Problems; Legal Problems; Mental Health; Personal Problems; Prison Probation; Recreation and Social Activities; Senior Citizens; Sex Related Concerns; Social Action; Transportation Problems and Services; and Veterans Services.
• Your local phone book also includes local government agency listings.
• Contact your local United Way.
• Contact your local Chamber Of Commerce to help place you, insist on it!
• Contact your local high school to find opportunities.
• Contact your House of Worship.
• Fill opportunities with national, staff hungry non-profit's that have local agencies, which are listed our database at ProjectSledgehammer.org/database.htm.

[ ]   CALL THE ORGANIZATION WHERE YOU WOULD LIKE TO VOLUNTEER.
• Contacting any organization is easy, simply identify yourself as a student of your high school or college or a specialist in your profession. Tell them what your curriculum or profession is. Tell them you would like to Career Volunteer, that you would like to do volunteer for work in your chosen career area and obtain actual involved experience with your field, and real world experience. Ask how they might fit your service around your schedule. The organization will probably do the rest of the talking and have some interesting opportunities with responsibility for you, since they usually always lack manpower.
• They'll probably ask you to stop by. High school and college students should treat it like a job interview for practice. Usually the first organization you select will accept you. If not, change your approach, keep changing your approach and select similar organizations to contact as if you were looking for a job. Ask until... Remember to ask for the level of responsibility you desire. And

remember, the few minutes you take here to make the initial phone call and interview can absolutely be a step towards positive change.

[ ]   BUILD YOUR EXPECTATIONS. SET A GOAL. WRITE IT DOWN. USE THE GOAL SETTING FORMAT BELOW, AND TAKE ACTION.
• Here are some questions to think about... When can I get started? How can I Career Volunteer to get ahead, while enjoying the process? What can I really do here to be proud of? How can I treat others as I would like to be treated? How much higher could I raise my self-confidence by helping others and uniting in my community? How would it feel if I introduce Career Volunteering to three of my friends? What will it cost me if I don't have resume experience and real world experience after I graduate? Lastly, without pain and sacrifice we would be nothing 1; am I nothing or will I evolve and contribute?
• Volunteer and look to yourself as a hero.

[ ]   GOAL SETTING GUIDELINE
To: (your name)
From: (myself)
Date: (year of, month of , or week of)
Subject: (Top 6 goals to achieve)
• All we do to plan our time is list and prioritize our top 6 goals once year, and break them down into what we need to do monthly, and then what action to take weekly. Our top 6 weekly goals are the small victories to get us where we want in a month, and then in a year. Keep your personal goals to yourself, and let your actions do the talking. Succeed with deeds not words.
• And if our actions aren't producing the desired result, we need to change our approach and keep changing our approach until it works because in the real world, winning isn't graded on a curve, and isn't based on luck. Winning happens when constant preparation meets opportunity. So take five minutes Monday morning to plan your weekly memo, and make a commitment to follow through. 21
• Please take our online survey at ProjectSledgehammer.org/surveys.htm, so that we are credited for the referral. Or take our survey that is listed at the end of this book, tear it out and mail it to us. Also remember to mark down a Career Volunteering section on your resume.

[ ]   START A PROJECT SLEDGEHAMMER GROUP
• Become a Project Sledgehammer Leader. Mentor others in or out of your curriculum to Career Volunteer as a group. Enjoy the process. Do the work. Have fun in your group.
• See Chapter Eight.

Career Volunteering Survey

Career Volunteer, Take This Survey, Tear Out & Mail It To:

Career Volunteering, Inc.
Mark Stefanick
P.O. Box 35
Crabtree, PA 15624

Name_____ Email_____

Address_____ City/State/Zip_____

Major/Field_____ Your School _____

1. Did you perform Career Volunteering type volunteering?
___ Yes

If you participate on a separate occasion in the future again, please make sure to take our survey again. If you have not, please go back and find more information to participate.

2. Name of the Non-profit where you career volunteered?

3. How many total hours did you career volunteer?
___1 ___2 ___3 ___4 ___5 ___10 ___15 ___20 ___25 ___30

___35 ___40 ___45 ___50 ___60 ___70 ___80 ___90 ___100 ___110

___120 ___150 ___200 ___250 ___300 ___350 ___400 ___450 ___500

4. Did you start a Project Sledgehammer group?
___ Yes

These very important results must be reported to our supporting grant makers. Thank you much.

Bibliography

1 Chuck Palahniuk and 20th Century Fox, FIGHT CLUB

2 Second Amendment Sisters, Inc., www.2asisters.org

3 Rich Geib, www.rjgeib.com

4 www.Wikipedia.org

5 Matthew White, http://users.erols.com/mwhite28

6 THE RETURN OF THE KING, Lyrics by Jules Bass

7 Rush, Subdivisions, SIGNALS

8 Rage Against the Machine, Settle For Nothing, RAGE AGAINST THE MACHINE

9 Ho Yen-his and Sun Tzu, THE ART OF WAR

10 THE AMERICAN HERITAGE® DICTIONARY OF THE ENGLISH LANGUAGE, 4th Edition

11 Rush, Losing It, SIGNALS

12 John R. Lott, Jr., MORE GUNS, LESS CRIME: UNDERSTANDING CRIME AND GUN CONTROL LAWS, SECOND EDITION

13 Nirvana, Smells Like Teen Spirit, NEVERMIND

14 Jon Linden, President, Proactive Intervention, L.L.C.

15 Wess Roberts, LEADERSHIP SECRETS OF ATTILA THE HUN

16 U2, Like a Song, WAR

17 Rush, Territories, POWER WINDOWS

18 Rush, Marathon, POWER WINDOWS

19 Tony Snow, FOX NEWS SUNDAY, FoxNews.com

20 Rage Against the Machine, Town Rebellion, RAGE AGAINST THE MACHINE

21 Friend and wireless industry entrepreneur Dan Cronin

22 THE PATRIOT

23 Stone Temple Pilots, Vaseline, PURPLE

24 Charlotte Thomson Iserbyt, the deliberate dumbing down of america

25 Peter Gabriel, Steam, US

26 Jeff Sartain, MICRO-FILM, The Parallel View, Pt. 1, One View: OUR LADY OF SORROW

ISBN 141200527-2